Who Said School Administration Would Be Fun?

Second Edition

This book is dedicated to my sons, Mark and
Joel, their partners, Shannon and Molly, and my two
granddaughters, Audrey and Stella, and to the women
in my family who have been educators before me—my
mother, Ercel; my aunt, Agnes; and my grandmother, Anna.

Who Said School Administration Would Be Fun?

COPING WITH A NEW EMOTIONAL AND SOCIAL REALITY

Jane L. Sigford

Second Edition

CORWIN PRESS
A SAGE Publications Company
Thousand Oaks, California

For information:

Corwin Press
A Sage Publications Company
2455 Teller Road
Thousand Oaks, California 91320
www.corwinpress.com

Sage Publications Ltd.
1 Oliver's Yard
55 City Road
London EC1Y 1SP
United Kingdom

Sage Publications India Pvt. Ltd.
B-42, Panchsheel Enclave
Post Box 4109
New Delhi 110 017 India

Printed in the United States of America

Library of Congress Cataloging-in-Publication Data

Sigford, Jane L.
Who said school administration would be fun?: Coping with a
new emotional and social reality / Jane L. Sigford.— 2nd ed.
    p. cm.
Includes bibliographical references and index.
ISBN 1-4129-1552-X (cloth) — ISBN 1-4129-1553-8 (pbk.)
    1. School management and organization—United States.
2. School administrators—United States. I. Title.
LB2805.S54 2005
371.2′00973—dc22   2004028779

This book is printed on acid-free paper.

05   06   07   08   09   10   9 8 7 6 5 4 3 2 1

Acquisitions Editor:	Elizabeth Brenkus
Editorial Assistant:	Candice L. Ling
Production Editor:	Beth A. Bernstein
Copy Editor:	Gillian Dickens
Typesetter:	C&M Digitals (P) Ltd.
Proofreader:	Kris Bergstad
Indexer:	Teri Greenberg
Cover Designer:	Rose Storey

Contents

Preface

To paraphrase M. Scott Peck in *The Road Less Travelled,* "Being a principal is difficult." The purpose of this book is to speak to those who are thinking of becoming an administrator and to support those who are already in the profession. For newcomers, it is hoped that it will help lead to understanding of the socioemotional pieces of the job that were not discussed in university programs for training administrators.

For experienced administrators, the book may affirm and clarify why some things happen as they do. The book is unique in that the literature does not deal with socioemotional aspects of the profession. As more nontraditionals, such as women and people of color, enter the profession, and because the demands placed on school leaders have changed, the necessary style of leadership has changed. Schools are forced to be more collegial within the organization and with the community at large. It is hoped that the rigid hierarchy is softening to incorporate more collaborative, shared leadership. However, as long as there are administrators who supervise others, it will be important for those leaders to understand the unspoken, unwritten rules. Many books are written about the positive aspects of administration, but they neglect the socioemotional, human elements that are surprising to practitioners. For some people, it is those aspects that make or break them as a successful or content administrator.

Administrators have obviously been successful learners. Training programs have provided instruction in learning theory, pedagogical strategies, and management needs. However, it is one thing to learn *about* something and another to *apply* those ideas in a human organization and understand the human responses. Much like an iceberg, where most of the ice is underwater and unseen, the socioemotional components of administration are rarely, if ever, described and discussed.

My own career journey has taken a rich path from classroom teacher to special education teacher, staff development trainer, and administrator, both at building and central office levels. The experiences have been in different districts. My educational preparation and doctoral research led me wonder why the psychosocial aspects of training are omitted. My doctoral research allowed me the opportunity to probe this dimension with the women who were head principals of high schools in Minnesota. In 1993–1994, there were only 26, a mere 5.6% of the total.

The words of these unique people and my experience led me to the realization that many socioemotional aspects of administration were not part of the formal training required for licensure. Women and persons of color are still nontraditional in the position of high school principal. In fact, because the population of students of color is growing faster than the numbers of adults of color in the profession, the gap is growing between the numbers of students of color and teachers/administrators of color.

ACKNOWLEDGMENTS

The author and Corwin Press gratefully acknowledge the contributions of the following individuals:

Albert Armer, Principal
Wortham Elementary School
Wortham, Texas

Janine Jellander, Assistant
    Principal
Agoura High School
Agoura Hills, California

Michelle Kocar, Principal
Liberty Elementary School
North Ridgeville, Ohio

Kathy Malnar, Superintendent
Hudson Area Schools
Hudson, Michigan

Ann Porter, Retired Principal
Lewis & Clark Elementary
    School
Grand Forks, North Dakota

Gina Segobiano,
    Superintendent/Principal
Signal Hill School District 181
Belleville, Illinois

Dana Trevethan, Principal
Turlock High School
Turlock, California

About the Author

Jane L. Sigford is the Executive Director of Curriculum and Instruction for the Wayzata Public Schools in Wayzata, Minnesota, a suburb of Minneapolis. Prior to this, she has been a high school principal in a suburban high school, an assistant principal at an urban high school in St. Paul (Minnesota), dean of students, an English teacher, a special education teacher, and a staff development trainer. She helped create a drop-in center for divergent learners at a suburban high school.

Sigford has been Adjunct Professor for the University of St. Thomas and Hamline University in St. Paul, Minnesota. She has a BS in English from Bemidji State University, Bemidji, Minnesota, and a MA from San Diego State University in English with a concentration on Black literature. Her certifications in teaching students with learning disabilities and in teaching students with emotional/behavioral disabilities are from the University of St. Thomas, St. Paul, Minnesota. She obtained her PhD in educational policy and administration from the University of Minnesota, Minneapolis.

She is the proud mother of two adult sons and proud mother-in-law as well. She is grateful for being part of the lives of her two granddaughters, Audrey and Stella, who give her great joy.

Introduction

O verall, this book deals with the inter- and intrapersonal issues a person must face as an administrator. Training programs deal with theories and the strategies of management. This book deals with the personal and emotional issues that we all face. An overarching theme throughout the book is about maintaining perspective by recognizing the paradoxes of our profession—and life in general.

Chapter 1 discusses the change of self-identity from teacher to administrator. Those stages resemble the stages of grief and loss as defined by Elizabeth Kubler-Ross.

Chapter 2 discusses the new paradigm of thinking about change within a system as a three-dimensional process, much like a fractal. It talks about how administrators act as change agents within an organization and whether their style meshes with their particular organization.

Chapter 3 talks about how a person fits with the culture of an organization.

Chapter 4 discusses communication patterns, particularly as they relate to different strategies to use with different groups.

Chapter 5 is about time management and the need for flexibility. An administrator must change the definition of a job well done because there are so many interruptions before tasks can be completed.

Chapter 6 is about how to maintain the paradox of emotional involvement and yet maintain a certain healthy distance. One suggestion is given for how to reframe issues so that they do not become so overwhelming.

Chapter 7 is about conflict—how it is a natural interaction of humans and how to deal with it. There are different strategies in dealing with different levels of conflict.

Chapter 8 helps administrators understand adult learners and the differences among generations. As administrators, we deal with adults as learners frequently. In addition, our staffs are composed of four generations of workers, all with their own style. It is helpful to have a framework for thinking about the adults in our workplace.

Chapter 9 is about maintaining perspective through the use of humor. Paradox is seen throughout the book. Humor uses paradox and irony to help us see the human side of the profession.

Chapter 10 is about power and control. Paradox is apparent when one thinks of the need to give away both power and control. The more one gives away, the more one has.

Chapter 11 is about accountability. Our current political climate is all about accountability. The topic is both fruitful and frightening.

Chapter 12 concludes with an overall look at how to become a self-assured administrator.

My hope is that the book will be a vehicle for self-reflection and conversation among peers to discuss the socioemotional aspects of being a school leader.

**CORWIN
PRESS**

The Corwin Press logo—a raven striding across an open book—represents the union of courage and learning. Corwin Press is committed to improving education for all learners by publishing books and other professional development resources for those serving the field of K–12 education. By providing practical, hands-on materials, Corwin Press continues to carry out the promise of its motto: **"Helping Educators Do Their Work Better."**

CHAPTER ONE

Why Is It So Chilly in the Teachers' Lounge?

W e know the importance of administrators. We know that it is important for successful schools—whether it is in academic success or in creating healthy school cultures and collaborations with communities—to have an instructional leader guiding the educational process. There is more to do than can ever possibly be done.

Whatever path someone takes to become an administrator— whether it is through the teaching ranks or from outside of education, whether someone has had years of teaching experience or none—there is a new adventure waiting. Administration is a rare opportunity to marry leadership and followership, creativity and redundancy, and scholar and manager.

Different states have different rules about requirements for administrative licensure. Some states require teaching experience, and others do not. Some require a certain number of years of teaching, and others do not. Whatever path a person chooses, whatever college major a person has, and whatever level of experience, whether elementary or secondary, the position of administrator offers some unique changes for the individual in self-identity and socioemotional discoveries.

1

Richard DuFour and Robert Eaker (1998), in their book *Professional Learning Communities at Work: Best Practices for Enhancing Student Achievement,* stated, "Strong principals [administrators and teacher leaders] are crucial to the creation of learning communities, but the image of how a strong principal operates needs to be reconsidered" (p. 183). Most administrators would probably aspire to be the "Level 5" leader as described by Jim Collins (2001) in his book *Good to Great.* A Level 5 leader is a paradoxical mix that is "modest and willful, humble and fearless" (p. 22). The leader has a "compelling modesty" (p. 27) and creates an organization that cultivates that type of leadership in others (p. 39).

DuFour and Eaker (1998, pp. 184–188) describe this leader as someone who

Leads through shared vision and values rather than through rules and procedures

Involves faculty members in the school's decision-making processes and empowers individuals to act

Provides staff with the information, training, and parameters they need to make good decisions

However, schools are hierarchical and bureaucratic. The instructional leader has to marry the instructional role with the necessary pieces of manager and supervisor to keep an organization running smoothly. It is an artistic endeavor to balance the roles.

TEACHERS AND ADMINISTRATORS

The bureaucratic, hierarchical structure of schools has created a series of subgroups that compete for scarce resources, attention, and power. Memberships within subgroups create subcultures with peculiar personal and professional realities. Although being part of a group creates a sense of belonging, it paradoxically creates a "we/they" culture among the groups within the organization.

One of the most powerful struggles within a school is the we/they thinking between teachers and administrators. Contentious struggles between union leaders and administration accent this separation. If union negotiations do not go well, the division is widened.

Teachers perpetuate the separation by having lounge and hallway conversations about administrators. "If only the principal. . . . If only the superintendent. . . ." Common, almost mantra-like criticisms are that principals are distanced from students, do not follow through on discipline, and are out of the building too much.

Administrators perpetuate the divide by having similar conversations, generalizing about "all" teachers, withholding information from teachers, or being removed from the daily work of classrooms.

There are two major reasons that the separation remains despite collaborative efforts. First, few teachers have been administrators and, therefore, cannot understand that role. Administrators have a more global viewpoint than do classroom teachers. Administrators must create a system where all parts interact and run smoothly, from transportation to food service, to special education to regular instruction. They are middle managers who must be a liaison between parents and community, teachers and parents, and building and superintendent.

However, the main concern for teachers is student achievement. Their world is more centered on classroom- and building-level concerns. Because they have never been an administrator, they, understandably, do not grasp the complexities of the administrative role. Administrators are often the intermediary between teachers and parents, as well as teachers and community, much more than teachers realize. Ironically, the more that an effective administrator keeps interference away from the classroom, the less likely it is that a teacher knows this is occurring.

Second, administrators remain as supervisors and evaluators of teachers. No matter how much collaboration is established within a school, anytime there is a power differential, there will be certain boundaries that cannot be crossed. It is not likely that someone can be a close personal friend with a subordinate. In fact, if a relationship level changes (e.g., by two people marrying), the supervisory responsibilities in a healthy organization are given to someone else. For example, if a principal marries a staff member, the evaluative responsibilities are given to the assistant principal.

As a teacher, one is part of the largest subgroup in the educational organization. As an administrator, one is part of the smallest and most scrutinized subgroups. However, administrators tend to have more power than other groups.

THE REALIZATION PROCESS

When someone leaves a subgroup, such as the group of teachers, and becomes part of management, such as educational administration, there must also be a change in the socioemotional realities and self-perception. For the new identity to be adopted successfully, one must experience stages of change and develop coping skills.

The first few weeks of the new job are exciting and unsettling. Because a person has had administrative classes, has earned a degree or certificate, and has been part of school systems, it is assumed that the person knows how to be an administrator. However, that is not entirely true. It is also assumed that head principals have had assistant experience to learn the job. That, too, is not always true. In my research, 35% of the women in the study became head principals directly out of the classroom, without benefit of interning, mentoring, or assistant principal experiences.

If someone begins an administrative career as an assistant principal, the head principal is responsible for offering guidance and direction. Unfortunately, the head principal is the one who has the least amount of time to do that. What usually happens is that the head principal offers overall structure and assumes that the assistant will be self-directed and motivated to "discover" the realities of the job. Once again, the structure of education is such that we do not get the opportunity to benefit fully from others' experiences. We do not have extended internships like the medical profession, where experienced doctors conduct "rounds" to question and teach. In education, we are too often on our own. As assistants, we are lucky to have conversations with the head principal "on the fly," in passing in the halls, or in short team meetings once a week. This is not enough.

Some administrators rise through the ranks from within their own organization, and others come from another district. Some even come from outside of education. Although some people make the transition with relative ease, most who leave teaching to become administrators describe a separation process from their former identity. They realize that their former teacher-friends are reserved around them. One woman described the isolation as follows: "There is no one to trust. No one at my level—I can't be friendly with staff" (Sigford, 1995, p. 132). Such words reflect the loneliness and painfulness of being "at the top" where there are few peers from whom to draw support.

Walking into the staff lounge as an administrator is a different experience from walking in as a teacher. The atmosphere feels chilly. Conversations stop or suddenly take a different direction. As one woman described it, "The definition [of you] changes as you get up in the organization. I don't sit and have coffee in the lounge anymore" (Sigford, 1995, p. 130). There is not the casual interaction in the hallways that there once was. Conversation in the office rarely crosses professional boundaries. Administrators and teachers may discuss family and personal interests, but it occurs on a different level. Teachers are more hesitant in their relationships with administrators because there is a power differential. A principal said, "I know I have people who care about me a lot, including my assistant principals and teachers, but I'm still the boss. There is a limit as to how close you can get" (Sigford, 1995, p. 130).

It is appropriate that there is a type of distance between administrators and teachers. It is difficult enough to supervise adults, but it is extremely difficult to supervise or discipline friends. Administrators must maintain care and concern for their staff but also must maintain a professional distance. One administrator described that she interacts frequently with her middle school staff. She goes to plays with them once a year as a faculty outing, and she goes to Friday after-school sessions. But she goes early and leaves early. Just as in healthy families, it is important for there to be respectful boundaries and clarity aligned with positions.

Even with the excitement and promise of a new position, with the change in role and self-identity, there is rightfully a sense of loss. People assume that moving up the ladder and taking a new position will be a joyful occasion, but they are surprised by and unprepared for the sadness and loneliness that are also there.

STAGES OF CHANGE FOR THE PERSONAL GROWTH PROCESS

In any major change, professional or personal, there is a growth process that one must go through to redefine the self. This change process is reminiscent of the grief process as described by Elizabeth Kubler-Ross (1969) in her book, *On Death and Dying.*

Kubler-Ross's work with terminally ill patients and with families who lost their loved ones led her to describe five stages of grief and loss. Each stage has a purpose and has lessons that must be learned. It is important to realize that the stages apply to a change, no matter if the change is perceived as positive or negative, because with any major change there is a loss, as well as a gain. Too often, people are not prepared for that paradox. For example, if a person moves to a new city, that is a good thing, but it also means leaving the familiar behind—the friends, restaurants, and familiar patterns. If a person starts a new job, there are new adventures ahead, but there is the loss of leaving known expectations, routines, and people behind. This is a type of loss.

Some people have gone through major life events but have not perceived this sense of loss. Change and loss affect people differently. Some are more attuned, whereas some could experience the loss of both parents but not experience these stages. As a therapist, Alla Bozarth-Campbell (1982), in her book *Life Is Goodbye, Life Is Hello,* clarified that

> what to one person may be a grievous loss may amount to mere inconvenience for another. The key is in the meaning which a person invests in what has been given up or taken away by fate, circumstances, or will. . . . The more of myself I have invested, given over, or entrusted outside of myself . . . in being cut off . . . from that part of me that the other represented . . . I have lost a part of my own self. (p. 25)

She further states that it is important "to discover the nature of the losses and their meanings and the impact of the feelings within ourselves, and then to find appropriate ways of responding. There are no short cuts" (p. 16).

Denial

Kubler-Ross (1969) calls this first stage *denial* because the person involved may deny the significance of the change. In a professional change, the first stage, denial, lasts about three to six months. If the change is a promotion, this first stage may feel like euphoria. If the change is a lateral move or demotion, the person in this stage may feel numb. When one leaves teaching to become an administrator, this denial stage is manifested in some startling "ahas." One is that the title *administrator* or *principal* has more credibility and authority in the eyes of students, staff, and parents. The words of an administrator are seen as more powerful than the words of a teacher.

Another "aha" is that the newness of the position prevents active processing in dealing with the reality of the loss. The new tasks, new people, and even a new office are exciting and different. This excitement masks the loss of what is no longer available, such as the easy camaraderie and support among teachers, a larger number of support persons, and the feeling of belonging to a large group identified with being a teacher.

The loss of identity and support is particularly keen for those nontraditionals in the field, such as women and persons of color. There are few peers to seek out. As one woman said, "Now I'm in a glass bowl. People watch carefully. They might misinterpret. There are not a lot of people to talk to" (Sigford, 1995, p. 130).

Part of the denial is that people have difficulty in changing their identity from teacher to administrator. They still think of themselves as teachers, denying that they are any different from when they were teachers. After all, they have been in a classroom and understand what that is like.

However, it only takes the first unpopular decision for the shift in self-identity. The administrator quickly becomes the "they" in the we/they culture of teacher and administration. For the sake of the administrator, the quicker one changes the mind-set to become an administrator, the quicker one can become successful in the role. One cannot maintain a dual identity because too many conflicts arise.

In one case, a new administrator clung to the identity that she was a teacher. For example, she forced the incorporation of using a reading series that she had used as a classroom teacher. She constantly referred to her teaching experiences. However, the teachers in her building did not expect her to act as a teacher; they wanted her to be an administrator. She struggled for two years but was never able to change her identity within that building. She left to become a principal in another district, was able to start over, and did not make that mistake. She currently is doing well but always describes herself as administrator.

The identity switch is forced rapidly after the first unpopular decision; conversations suddenly change when the administrator walks by in the hall. Fewer people drop by the office just to chat. People start making appointments to share their opinion—"just so that you know." Staff members go out on Friday after school and invite the administrator occasionally, but the conversations are different because the administrator cannot be entirely relaxed and candid in conversations. There is an emotional distance that was not there previously. The reality of the position begins to set in.

Anger

Anger, the second stage, surfaces when teachers and administrators have differing opinions. It is startling for a new administrator the first time there is a difference of opinion with teachers. As an administrator, one expects to have differing opinions with parents and students, but it is startling to realize the number of times it happens with teachers. Because teachers do not have the same vantage point as administrators, they assume that everyone works as hard as they do and follows policy and procedures. They do not realize how many times an administrator has to hold teachers accountable.

Dealing with staff issues is one of the most difficult parts of being an administrator. As a former teacher, an administrator expects people to do their jobs and to do them well. It is disheartening, and part of the grief, when that does not occur. This disillusionment causes frustration and anger.

It is particularly irksome that staff do not have an inkling of the turmoil of administration. It is easy for teachers to sit in the lounge and criticize, but administrators cannot share complete explanations because of professional boundaries and data privacy. An administrator sometimes thinks, "If only they knew. . . ."

One way to deal with the anger is to blame others. But in healthy organizations, "Level 5" leaders (Collins, 2001) use a window and mirror approach. When things go well, the leader looks out the window to attribute success to the staff. When things do not go well, the leader looks into the mirror to accept responsibility (pp. 33–35).

Schools are complex systems with complex interactions. It is important at this point to understand that feelings of anger and frustration are a normal *evolution* from teacher to administrator and not a *result*. If the administrator is to be successful, the anger will dissipate, as the reflective administrator is able to monitor the process of change.

Bargaining

When the rosy feeling of the new job is over and the anger has surfaced, it is time to progress to the third stage of *bargaining.* One begins to identify with the position of administration and crosses the divide from the personal journey to the professional one. The person begins to leave the old role behind.

Some principals begin practicing things they have studied during this time. For example, one principal said she would improve her listening. She wanted to help "key leaders from the building . . . work hard at having people confront issues, not talk behind people's backs" (Sigford, 1995, p. 122).

Another principal used a "lot of brainstorming and sharing. It sometimes gets into shouting and arguing with each other but we work it out." One principal described it as "various groups . . . all have parts of a puzzle to look at. I try to get various groups to have ownership but not be bogged down" (Sigford, 1995, p. 122).

Bargaining is an unconscious part of the self-talk that occurs during this stage. "If I try this, people will view me as a successful administrator." "Administration has to do. . . ." The administrator begins to identify more with conversations from the central office than those in the teachers' lounge. The journey toward the professional administrator has begun. "There is more to be seen than can be seen."

Depression

The fourth stage, *depression,* may be disguised as frustration, exhaustion, and stress. It can be characterized by self-doubt. It is at this point that some administrators think about leaving to return to teaching, to move to a new district, or to pursue a career in other areas, such as curriculum, college teaching, or a superintendency. The faulty assumption is that any of those positions would be less stressful. Despite the difficulties and complexities of administration, few people return to teaching. Because administration has a more global perspective of education and different opportunities to make a difference, and teaching is so proscribed, it is difficult to return to the classroom.

Some people leave during this stage because the job is hard; it does not feel good. Some people want to feel the euphoria of the newness of Stage 1 all over again. They become "change junkies" because of that initial "high." Unfortunately, depression is the next stage after bargaining, no matter what the change or what job a person has. If one gets a new job and a new "high," the next stage will come eventually.

Depression is common, especially toward the end of the second year. The honeymoon is over, bargaining did not work entirely, and the job is difficult. It is important to realize that this stage is necessary and unavoidable. There is personal work to be done within this stage to achieve the more peaceful place of success. For some people, this stage is short-lived and barely recognizable, but it does occur.

Acceptance

The final stage, *acceptance*, becomes apparent when one realizes a feeling of ownership and pride as an administrator. It often takes from three to five years to achieve this. There is a feeling of satisfaction in making a difference in the lives of students and staff. There is awareness that one has been able to make a change. Disagreements with staff, parents, and students no longer feel personal. It is as though there is a Plexiglas shield around the body so that one can see and deal with issues, but the issues cannot cause personal damage. Certainly, there will always be discouraging days, but the problems do not seem unsolvable. Plus, some of the problems are repeats, and the administrator has built up a databank of resolutions. "Oh, I've done this before. I can handle this." It is like making the master schedule for the second time. The first time feels fragmented, complex, and intimidating. The second time is easier, and by the third time, one is a pro and can even preempt some of the problems. It is like making classroom assignments for elementary classrooms to make sure that the classes are balanced male/female, gifted/not gifted, special ed/ regular ed. It gets easier each time.

The job is difficult. Not everyone will agree with what an administrator does all the time. In fact, if no one disagrees, a person wonders if there is something wrong. Plus, it seems that an administrator will hear the "naysayers" first, and the positive voices will always come later.

It is a milestone of acceptance when an administrator can walk into the teachers' lounge and describe the atmosphere as "removed," not chilly. Administrators are indeed removed from the role of teachers. That is part of the acceptance of the position.

GETTING STUCK

Each stage of change has a purpose and a lesson that must be learned before the process can be completed. Sometimes, people get stuck in a stage. They create situations in which they repeat a stage over and over, rather than dealing with issues so they can move on.

Some people like the euphoria of the first stage. For example, when a person accepts a new job, there is exhilaration. When some of the struggles of the new job begin to set in, however, some people may actually change jobs rather than feel the pain and work through the process. By avoiding the pain, they end up re-creating the same situation over and over. They move from job to job or district to district to feel the excitement, rather than staying long enough to feel the not-so-positive feelings.

Others recreate job situations where they are stuck in anger. They are angry about how hard they work in comparison to other people. When their job starts going better, they will create a situation so they can feel angry once more. They are recognizable by their language because they are always blaming someone else when the job becomes overly stressful—teachers, superintendents, parents, school boards, students. They seem to hate their job.

Physically, anger is like love, in that it produces endorphins in the body. Some people are just as addicted to the endorphins of anger as others are addicted to the "high" produced by exercise and laughter. They become "anger junkies."

Some people get stuck in the third stage, bargaining. They never get to the point of self-assurance and identity as an administrator. They never give up the role of teacher entirely. They are not able to live with the unpopularity of decisions and constantly try to appease all factions, an impossible task. They have difficulty defining the bottom line. They believe to a fault that if they work harder and smarter, all will be well.

Others are stuck in depression. They feel that the world, their friends, their training, and even life in general, have failed them. They wallow in self-pity and blame everyone else for their discomfort. If something starts going well, they will put a negative slant to it. Nothing will ever be good enough. The world is a cup half empty.

The final stage, acceptance, is a pleasant place to be stuck. It takes time to achieve this level. This is not to say that there are not days of denial, anger, bargaining, or depression, but, overall, the administrator has achieved an understanding of the position, the self, and the balance and interaction between the two. In Collins's (2001) terms, is this a Level 5 leader?

The Work of Each Stage

Each stage has tasks that must be accomplished successfully before moving forward. The work of the first stage, *denial,* is to help separation and redefinition. The work of this time is to eliminate those things that are no longer necessary. A person experiences *letting go.* This stage helps by pruning the unnecessary remnants of the past to help define what is necessary to carry forward into the new.

Hanging onto the label *teacher* is one example of denial. Administrators are still teachers but in a very different sense. The instruction is more likely to be procedural or process learning, particularly because administrators are working with adult learners who have very different needs from those of children.

Administrators are also more likely to teach one-on-one or in small groups, as opposed to classroom instruction. Teacher evaluations are an example. Conferencing with a teacher to improve instruction is an administrator's type of teaching. Although it is vastly different from standing in front of a classroom of 25 six-year-olds, it is equally powerful. It is more removed from students but may have more of an impact because as an administrator influences teachers, the teachers, in turn, influence hundreds of students. Although administrators continue to instruct, their role is to be an administrator. It is important to accept that.

The work of the second stage, *anger,* is to facilitate the separation from the former position to the present one. Unless there is a good reason to let go, people have a tendency to cling to old ideas and identities. Leaving something behind is painful, and it can make someone sad or angry. For some people, it feels stronger to leave angry rather than to experience the pain of sadness. However, it is important to realize that anger is a cover-up emotion because it masks the pain of fear and sadness.

An example of the purpose of anger is illustrated by a story that I have told seniors in high school when they become depressed and angry in the spring of their senior year. The senior year has been publicized as wonderful and exciting, and many students are unprepared for the roller coaster of feelings that occur during that time. In reality, the senior year is difficult because of its many endings. The last basketball game. The last pep fest. The last dance. The pain is particularly prevalent around prom time because students might stay with their boyfriend or girlfriend through prom and break up immediately after. There are so many "lasts" during the year. What students do not know, because they have not lived long enough, is that there are many "firsts" waiting just around the corner.

Students get angry with their friends and significant others because it feels stronger and less vulnerable than feeling sad. They do not want to walk around crying all year because being sad feels helpless and weak. Therefore, students use anger to help them make separations and say goodbye.

Adults use the same mechanisms when they make major life changes. For example, few divorces end happily. Anger can help a person move forward as long as it helps separation. But it can be destructive if someone enjoys the feeling and refuses to leave it behind.

The task of the third stage, *bargaining,* is to begin fusing denial and anger to refocus on the future. The work of the first two stages is to say goodbye to the past. Bargaining is the bridge to the work of the future that brings together what was learned in the past to help shape the future. It is this fusion that helps create the new self-identity.

The fourth stage, *depression,* is necessary for the final letting go. If one cannot perform that final release, it is at this stage that a person will leave to take a new position. This stage often occurs around the end of the second year of administration. Working through the stages of grief and change are like experiencing a roller coaster ride. In depression, the roller coaster has taken a downturn again, almost like returning to the earlier stage of anger; that does not feel good. This is the final and crucial stage before one can move to a new socioemotional reality.

The final upturn of the ride comes with *acceptance,* occurring around the third to fourth year in the position. It takes that long for ideas to gel, for programs that were set in motion to demonstrate results, and for a person to change self-perception. Acceptance feels good.

We never learn about the emotional stages of change in graduate school. Professors tend to ignore discussing the socioemotional parts of the job because such discussions feel "soft." By the very nature of schools, we as administrators do not talk about such things with our peers because we are so isolated. We have little opportunity to be reflective as we deal with the daily task of survival. It is through the recognition and acceptance of the work of these stages, however, that helps administrators achieve successful socialization in their roles as administrators.

No one said change would be easy. The roller coaster effect is painful, but after every downturn, there is an upturn that ends, it is hoped, on a plateau. The height of the hills and valleys of the roller coaster ride diminishes with each succeeding stage. The important part of the process is to recognize the work that must be done. There are no shortcuts. But there are many rewards.

SUGGESTIONS FOR HOW TO DEAL WITH THE CHANGE PROCESS

1. To deal with change successfully, one must recognize that there are stages. Thich Nhat Hanh (1998) quotes the Buddha, who said, "When something has come to be, we have to acknowledge its presence and look deeply into its nature" (p. 31). Naming and describing the stages makes them less frightening. There will be backsliding within the stages, but the return to the more advanced stage will be shorter if the work inherent to the stage has been accomplished.

2. Learn to forgive if there is a return to a previous stage. There may be a return to anger or denial, but that is normal. Change is not a linear process. Just as in dieting, if there is a slip, do not give up. Just start again tomorrow.

3. Experience the stages; do not withdraw from them. Avoiding them means that they will appear in a different fashion and will have to be dealt with anyway. People have a tendency to avoid that which is painful, which is only a short-term solution for a long-term problem. Like the seniors in high school, one must experience all the endings so that one can rejoice in the new beginnings.

4. Look forward to the next stage. If one looks backward continually, one is likely to miss the scenery ahead.

5. Practice proactivity. Record this journey in some way, perhaps in a journal. Some may want to draw their journal. Others may keep an e-log. Others will write in a traditional fashion. It is helpful to have some record because it is amazing to read what has happened in a year. As one lives day to day, it is hard to see the pieces of the whole. Reading what happened a year ago is always astonishing because of the perspective it offers.

6. Find someone at a similar professional stage. Structure time together to discuss experiences. Free time is a luxury, but being able to find support is crucial. Join a principals' organization. Join Phi Delta Kappa. Start a study group within your district.

7. Do something outside of education. It is too easy to become single-minded. Find several things that transport mind and body away from education. Read "garbage" novels. Run. See plays. Bike. Walk in the woods. Golf. Fish. Watch the crackling fire in the fireplace. We give this good advice to our staff but do not always follow our own good suggestion. It is important for educational leaders to model this behavior.

8. Recognize that change is certain; growth is optional. Life will change and people will change. One can either be an active participant in the process, or one can be controlled by it.

Box 1.1   Journal

1. When did I experience the stages of change?

2. Where am I in my career?

3. What issues do I need to work on before I can move forward?

4. How can I use this information in my work with my staff?

5. What are "aha's" for me in this chapter?

CHAPTER TWO

Change Isn't a Flowchart

It's Broccoli

The previous chapter talked about the stages of *personal* change in working through the stages, which could be likened to stages of grief and loss. An administrator also has to understand the workings of *system* change. This chapter discusses change as a three-dimensional process and the ramifications of that complexity.

In the news each day, we hear about how life is changing rapidly. Although the words of William Strauss and Neil Howe (1997) were written before the terrorist attacks in the United States on September 11, 2001, they feel even more appropriate now:

> America feels like it's unraveling. . . . We have settled into a mood of pessimism about the long-term future, fearful that our superpower nation is somehow rotting from within. . . . The America of today feels worse, in its fundamentals, than the one many of us remember from youth. (p. 1)

These words feel even truer since the World Trade Towers were attacked.

We hear that our society is changing in population, with increasing diversity and a widening economic gap. We hear that schools must be accountable and that no child should be left behind.

We hear how families have changed, how students are coming to school less prepared than before. We hear how educational options are dictating that schools be more competitive for students.

Paradoxically, as technology and multinational companies have made the world seem like physical boundaries are outdated, we struggle even more to identify with different subgroups to get a sense of belonging. Instead of national citizenships, people are reestablishing their ethnic self-descriptions. Mary Pipher (2002), author of *The Middle of Everywhere: Helping Refugees Enter the American Community,* said that "our economy and our technology have changed much more rapidly than our conceptions about what it means to be human. In our rapidly changing world, we need research about the effects of global meld on people" (p. 305).

People in general—and teachers and administrators in particular—feel beleaguered by the changes in society and the increasing social and academic pressures on schools. The movements and demands are coming faster and more frequently with less time in between to catch our breath.

Consequently, teachers and administrators are under a great deal of stress. It is as though there is nothing that is constant; nothing is the same as it used to be. Neither our training nor our life experiences prepared us for the sense of fragmentation of the 21st century.

Tinkering With School Change

This chapter challenges the reader to reframe thinking about how change operates. In the past, change has been described as a linear process. Consequently, we have seen that in organizations such as schools, where that type of thinking was used to suggest change, deep change has not materialized. Therefore, I would challenge educational leaders to think about a new paradigm.

Larry Cuban coined the phrase "tinkering toward Utopia" in his book by the same title, written with David Tyack in 1995. The book averred that most educational "reform" efforts have been mere "tinkering" but not truly substantial reform efforts. In that same vein, Michael Fullan (1993), in *Change Forces: Probing the Depths of Educational Reform,* gave a brief synopsis of change efforts over the past 30-plus years. He agreed with Cuban because what has happened is "tinkering after all . . . on a small or large scale, its main characteristic being 'a clumsy attempt to mend something.'" What is crucial for administrators, new or experienced, to understand is that "we need a different formulation to get at the heart of the problem" (Fullan, 1993, p. 3).

One difficulty in doing that is the human element of fear, fear of change, and fear of the unknown. Unless the administrator and the organization itself understand this fear, "tinkering," not reform, will be the practice of the day.

Change Is Nonlinear and "Chaotic": In Fact, Change Is Like Broccoli

In researching and studying change, mostly to find out why something did not work, I have been led to studies by Margaret Wheatley (1994), author of *Leadership and the New Science,* and others who talked about chaos theory, change, and leadership. Chaos theory is a theory about process, rather than a state of being. "Chaos," says planning expert T. J. Cartwright, "is order without predictability" (Wheatley, 1994, p. 123). It is a study of whole dynamic systems, rather than individual parts. It is the study of how a small change in input can make a major change in output.

Chaos theory describes change as three-dimensional and less predictable than we have tried to make it. Elements of chaos theory—butterfly effect, fractals, and "strange attractors"—are important elements to understand to grasp the complexity of the change process. The *butterfly effect* refers to the power of a small change on an entire system. Edward Lorenz, a meteorologist, was using a computer simulation to try to predict weather. By making a minor adjustment in the data, equivalent to the flapping of a butterfly wing, major alterations in weather were created, and a "hurricane" developed halfway around the world. A small change produced a wide variation (Wheatley, 1994, p. 126).

How did that small change create such an effect? To understand that, one must understand the concept of "strange attractors." A strange attractor is an event, information, or a data point outside the normal system that creates novelty. "'Strange attractors' draw attention and lead the disrupted system into a new visible shape" (Wheatley, 1994, p. 122). At first, the pattern may not become visible and seems random, but "if we look at such a system long enough and with the perspective of time, it always demonstrates its inherent orderliness" (Wheatley, 1994, p. 21).

Fullan (1993) wrote that "chaos in a scientific sense is not disorder, but a process in which contradictions and complexities play themselves out coalescing into clusters" (p. 18). The flap of a wing becomes a strange attractor that draws energy to it and creates a new cluster.

Fullan (1993) states that "strange attractors do not guide the process (because it is not guidable), they capitalize on it" (p. 18). In my college statistics classes, a number that varied greatly from the rest was lopped off as an outlier a statistical anomaly. In chaos theory, that could have been the flap of a wing, a strange attractor that precipitates the beginning of a new pattern.

The strange attractor or flap of a butterfly's wing may be the disrupter of old patterns that leads to reshaping new patterns that have not been seen before. The terrorist attack on the World Trade Center on September 11, 2001, was a strange attractor, the flap of a butterfly's wing that created a context that will shape the world for years to come.

In education, some attractors may be the No Child Left Behind (NCLB) Act of 2001, the standards movement, and school choice. We do not know the shape of education that may result because we do not have enough data at this point.

Chaotic patterns become descriptive when enough data and events are fed into the system. "If the system is non-linear, iterations can take the system in any direction, away from anything we might expect" (Wheatley, 1994, p. 125). When we have enough time and enough reactions to the NCLB Act or school choice, for example, we will be able to see patterns emerge.

Paradoxically, chaos theory itself can be an outlier for how we perceive change efforts. In the past, we have thought of change as linear, rational, and orderly. However, we now have the idea of change as chaos theory. This idea is a strange attractor that draws energy and creates its own new, nonlinear pattern. Who knows what change will look like in the future?

Fractals

As a flap of butterfly wing creates a strange attractor that attracts energy over time, a new nonlinear pattern, called a fractal, becomes visible. Fractals are found in nature in such examples as the patterns of ferns, snowflakes, broccoli, and the coastline of the United States.

In the past, we have thought of fractals as patterns without order, as chaotic. However, with computer technology, which allows more input more quickly, we have been able to understand that there is an order, a three-dimensional order.

How do fractals relate to change? Because we have defined change as a two-dimensional, simplistic, linear model as opposed to a three-dimensional, chaotic model as represented by fractals, we have not been able to create systemic, lasting change.

We need to use three-dimensional models because we have more information about the complexities of human nature and organizations. To help the reader understand the idea, I will use a common fractal, broccoli, as an analogy.

1. Broccoli and change are fractals; therefore, they are chaotic in nature.

2. Broccoli and change are paradoxical.

3. Broccoli and change are three dimensional.

4. Broccoli and change are holograms.

5. Broccoli and change are synergistic, the system greater than its parts.

6. Broccoli and change are dynamic and nondeterministic.

7. Broccoli and change appear to be disorderly but instead describe orderliness in a new way.

One, a fractal is a geometric pattern that, no matter how small, reflects the shape of the whole. To help understand this concept, take broccoli apart. Keep breaking it down. The smallest piece looks like the whole.

Two, change and broccoli are paradoxical. Although broccoli appears to be random, unpredictable, and formless, we recognize it as broccoli. Change may seem random, but we can recognize it. Although deep change seems chaotic, given time and enough experience, we can describe it.

Three, broccoli and change are three dimensional. It is not easy to represent broccoli in a two-dimensional pattern. Nor is it easy to represent change efforts. In the past, we have drawn flow-charts, input/output diagrams, circles, and arrows to point out what is happening and where we are going. Our computers even have little buttons that will help draw automatic flowcharts. The physical two-dimensional structure of paper shaped our thinking because it demanded two-dimensional graphics. However, we can now draw three-dimensional models on computer screens (even though the screens are flat) in a manner that more appropriately imitates what happens in a change effort. The ability to think in three-dimensional formats helps us reshape our thinking about how to deal with change.

Four, broccoli and change are holograms, which means that the smallest piece looks like the larger piece. If one breaks the florets apart, the smallest piece looks like the larger broccoli, which is true of change initiatives as well. What happens on a large scale must also happen to the individual. If a system or insti-tution changes, the individuals within that system must change in like fashion.

An example is the implementation of accountability. Each teacher has to be accountable for demonstrating that each student is learning. In turn, the school has to make certain that all students are learning. With the national-level NCLB Act, dis-tricts and states are being held accountable in the same fashion as the individual teacher.

Five, broccoli and change are synergistic, building on them-selves, creating something greater than the sum of their parts, which can be a positive or negative force. A small piece of broccoli is not as powerful as the combination of roots, stalk, and florets. The entire plant, or the whole change effort, is not merely addi-tive; instead, it is geometrically different. So too with change. It is not just a few ideas here and there; it is the whole system that cre-ates something entirely different.

Knowing that the whole is greater than the sum of its parts allows us the ability to gather more information, be more resource-ful, and maybe even be more playful as we look to initiate or sustain change. In a change effort, we must honor the complexity of the system rather than try to name the parts.

For example, the NCLB Act is more than holding schools accountable. It is a new way to think of federal involvement in schools, of what and who defines academic progress, what rights parents have and what rights they will exercise, and so on. NCLB creates a new pattern, a complex pattern, that looks at the inter-action of parts to create something different from the mere additive sum of the parts.

Six, broccoli and change are dynamic and nondeterministic. When the seed begins to grow, no one can predict the precise shape of that broccoli plant. Plant growth depends on other factors such as nutrients available, sunlight, water, and so on. So too with change. We do not know what shape the effort will take.

Seven, broccoli and change appear to be disorderly but actually redefine their own order. We look at various stalks of broccoli and recognize them as broccoli. However, each plant is unique and defines its own order.

Likewise, we have no way of knowing how the accountability movement will drive—or not—changes in education. It may be that the NCLB Act is a "strange attractor" that creates a fractal-like change as it attracts energy to reshape education. It may be that from this movement, another idea is spawned that creates effects we have not even thought of. It is still too early to tell.

Thinking about change as a fractal helps us understand the nonlinear, complex, order-within-disorder nature of change. It helps alleviate the frustration of trying to predict cause and effects in a flowchart.

As Fullan (1993) said in *Change Forces: Probing the Depths of Educational Reform,* "Change is a journey not a blueprint. [It] is non-linear, loaded with uncertainty and excitement and sometimes perverse" (p. 21).

Change is difficult to predict because the effort itself is chaotic in terms of its fractal-like nature. In addition, organizations are fractals. Thinking of the permutations possible between two fractals, two three-dimensional, nonlinear systems, one realizes that no wonder is it difficult to predict and plan lasting, deep change efforts.

Organizations as Fractals

Phyllis Wheatley (1994), in *Leadership and the New Science: Learning About Organization From an Orderly Universe,* said that organizations are "fractal in nature," with the smallest unit reflecting the attitudes, beliefs, and behavior of the larger institution (p. 128).

How would it shape your thinking if you thought of your organization as a stalk of broccoli? How would you try to initiate a change effort?

A leader will think about how to influence the components of floret, stalk, and roots if envisioning change as a fractal. Directing goals on a site plan will not necessarily affect the roots. Providing information on student achievement to the "stalk," the staff and parents, will not necessarily mean that change will flow to the "roots" of the organization or to the "florets" where change can be effected.

How Does Change Occur Within a Fractal?

To answer the question of how change is created from one part of the fractal, or organization, to another, one must look at how a fractal is created mathematically. A fractal is the result of putting the solution of a nonlinear equation back into the original equation and plotting the points. Deriving the solution is not the end but merely the beginning of feeding this information back into the whole. Many bits of data are fed back.

Because the formula is nonlinear, the result is a beautiful, dynamic, three-dimensional object such as broccoli or a fern. "Since there can be no definitive measurement, what is important in a fractal landscape is to note the quality of the system—its complexity and distinguishing shapes, and how it differs from other fractals" (Wheatley, 1994, p. 129). Consequently,

> There is never a satisfying end to this reductionist search, never an end point where we finally know everything about even one part of the system. When we study the individual parts or try to understand the system through its *quantities,* we get lost in a world we can never fully measure nor appreciate. (Wheatley, 1994, p. 129)

To put the idea of a fractal equation into the terms of change within education, one should think of the equation as what we do in education. The "solutions" of the equation are information and relationships, which we feed back into the equation to create the "fractal" of change.

If all it takes is to have relationships and information and to feed that information back into the equation we call education, why is long-lasting, deep change so difficult to create in our system? The structure of schools as chaotic organizations is described by Bolman and Deal (1991) as "loosely coupled," meaning that the parts are loosely affiliated with the whole. There are many layers, many individuals who are self-contained, which makes it difficult to get information dispersed and relationships established. Teachers are in their classrooms by themselves. Administrators have infrequent, short interactions with staff on a daily basis and have staff meetings once a month to convey information.

Therefore, because of this fragmented nature of communication within the organization, it is difficult to create the depth of communication that will sustain the type of human interactions that are necessary to make an effective change process. We end up "tinkering," creating incremental, as opposed to fundamental, change, as defined by Cuban (2001) in *How Can I Fix It?*

Incremental changes are minor modifications to decrease "inefficiency and ineffectiveness of existing structures and cultures of schooling, including classroom teaching" (Cuban, 2001, p. 43). Fundamental change "alter[s] permanently" the structures that are "irretrievably flawed at their core and need a complete overhaul or replacement, not improvement" (Cuban, 2001, p. 44). However, many changes that were intended to be fundamental become "incrementalized" because so much work is involved to create the relationships and sustain the communication, and it is difficult to get the amount of data needed to create a systemic, deep change.

It was thought by some political leaders that school choice options would change public schools greatly, that choices would be the information in the equation that would cause the system to change.

Many states have choices for educational delivery such as charter schools or home schooling. However, one must realize that there is little or no opportunity for those involved in charter schools or even private schools to enter conversations among the systems. Public school people do not share with charters and vice versa. There is no way for the knowledge to be shared, and there is no way for relationships to be developed on any large scale. Therefore, there cannot be enough information fed into the system to cause change.

What may cause change, however, is an event that is occurring and could be defined as a strange attractor—school funding. It may be that funding—or lack of it—attracts enough energy to cause change in the larger system. We do not know yet because we do not have enough information.

Relationships are another way to feed information back into the equation and change the system. Healthy relationships are those that allow the free interchange of information. If information is constantly fed back into the system from many avenues, from floret, stalk, and roots, then the "plant" can change. If, however, the information and the relationships occur only on the surface, in the florets, the change will not permeate the rest of the organization. For example, Fullan (2001) says that "individual development combined with professional communities is still not sufficient, unless it is channeled in a way that combats the fragmentation of multiple innovations by working on *program coherence*" (p. 146).

Therefore, administrators who want to create deep change within an organization must consider the three-dimensional equation that needs information and relationships for change. Relationships must be established at all levels simultaneously so all parts receive the data. Think of how difficult that is to do. It is no wonder we do not see deep change within our system.

If we continue to play with incremental change, we will continue to use two-dimensional models. If we want fundamental change, we will treat change efforts and organizations as fractals.

Three Personality Types in Dealing With Change

Change is inevitable. Most of it is positive and productive, but that does not make its effects any less drastic, especially when one takes into consideration the stages that one must experience, as discussed in Chapter 1. It takes time to process.

How people deal with change is likely to fall into three categories.

1. A Type 1 person will jump on the bandwagon and adopt anything new because our culture says, "New is better." Some people like to be trendsetters; they like the "high" of doing new things— change "junkies."

2. A Type 2 person may resist change because it comes too fast. They change only when absolutely forced into it.

3. A Type 3 person uses a combination of approaches, sometimes changing readily and sometimes waiting.

To make a change within a school, administrators will have to understand their own personal style plus the styles of the staff in the building. To get a change initiative going, an administrator may use a Type 1 person to get something going, but will have to have some Type 3 people on board for the effort to succeed. The Type 1 people do not always have staying power, so it is important to get some energy around the initiative, particularly the staying energy. It is particularly helpful if the Type 1 individual is respected by the staff so that the Type 3 people are willing to look at the issue and support it. The Type 2 people will move only if forced, so be prepared to do so.

For example, a principal wants to start a new pre–advanced placement (AP) vertical teaming program at the middle level. It is important to start talking to teachers who are willing to look at new programs. It would be important to take some Type 1 and 3 people and maybe a Type 2 individual to a district that already is successful with vertical teams. Then ask for volunteers to be on a fact-finding committee to discuss issues. It is hoped that Type 1 and strong Type 3 people will volunteer. If they go forward, the team will devise an implementation plan with the necessary professional development schedule. Usually, such teams ask for volunteers. As the principal gets the list for the 3-year plan, the Type 2 people will be on Year 3, with the hopes that the effort will have passed by then. It is important to understand the three-dimensional aspects of this effort to proceed.

It is important to understand the personal effect that change has on people. Think about the stages as described in Chapter 1. Remember that staff members are not only experiencing change in their professional lives but in their personal lives as well. Humans need a certain constancy in their lives. When persons have a lot of change in their personal lives, they may want their professional lives to be stable. When their professional lives are in flux, they may want stability in their personal lives. If both areas are in turmoil, a person is likely to be severely stressed and may be ineffectual in both. Bernie Siegel (1998), author of *Love, Medicine, and Miracles*, wrote that extreme stress could lead to illness and/or accidents. It is important to know that some people are resistant because they fear change. They prefer doing what is comfortable because change means going through stages of loss, as described previously.

To facilitate change, an administrator must understand the stages, how individuals approach the stages in their own idiosyncratic fashion, and then an administrator must support individuals as they wend their throught the process.

Levels of Change

There are different levels of change within a building. First, there are the changes that come from external organizations, such as the district office, the state department of educations, and school boards. Such mandates are usually carried out to some degree. For example, districtwide testing has to be completed. The new process requires that for each of their homeroom students, teachers must make certain that all tests are completed with each student's name and number. If the teacher does not check that this is done accurately, someone else, usually a counselor, must do it. The counselor is overwhelmed because instead of checking 20 papers, there are hundreds.

At this level, the thinking is that this is "not my job." "This is not why I went into teaching/administration." Because some teachers see this as one more thing they have to do, particularly as a noncurriculum chore, they resent being told what to do and will perform their task only minimally. They think the process should be as it was in the past, when the counselors were responsible for making sure the forms were accurately marked. Even though this is a relatively small change, teachers resist because it is "just one more thing." It is the task of administrators to deal with the resistance, but remember that too many of these interferences undermine the morale of a staff. If possible, minimize these directives.

Changes that come from external sources, such as legislatures and departments of education, have a tendency to generate skepticism from teachers. The force initiating the change seems faceless and nameless. When there is no relationship and little information (keeping in mind the discussion about change as a fractal that requires both information and relationships), it is no wonder that not much changes, and, if anything does, it is with minimal compliance.

Another level is change in curricula and instructional delivery systems. This level affects individual teachers more directly because it is a combination of external force and internal need. There is that necessary relationship and information for change to occur. The change is more meaningful and has immediacy. To make change happen, administrators must make their efforts useful so that the needs of our adult learners as constructivists are met.

A third level is internal change that is created by personal needs. A teacher develops a new unit because there is a better way to get information to students. Teachers seek out professional development on designing formative assessments so they can monitor the academic progress of individual students more handily. From the perspective of adult learners, this change happens because the need affects the adult directly. The adult is self-motivated, not externally motivated. The barriers to learning are down because the teacher sees it as a priority. To get effective change, an administrator needs to try to create situations where third-level change occurs for most of the staff members.

Tasks of an Administrator in the Change Process

The primary function of the administrator is to set the focus and direction of the building. The efforts that support that direction may come from a variety of sources. Ideas often come from the staff to the administration. A good administrator sets change in motion, then gets out of the way and lets professionals do their job.

The second task of the administrator is to be the cheerleader and support the change. Being a good supporter means that the administrator has to recognize where the effort is on the change timeline. Do the organizers need support, new ideas, or praise? Are they in the first year? Second? Third? Is it time for those involved to promote their efforts publicly?

The third task is to give recognition publicly and privately to those who are working hard. A good administrator will never take credit for the work of others. Public recognition has the function of exciting those on the outside to encourage them to join in, and it helps affirm the efforts of those involved.

The fourth task is to build in continuity. Many administrators do not stay in their positions long enough to see their efforts mature. Teachers will be resistant to expending effort if they do not believe that there will be support for their efforts over a period of time. So if the commitment is to be a change agent, it is important to commit to the long-term process. It is important to recognize the three-dimensional aspects of the change process and to give enough information and build relationships to create deep change.

Organizational Fit for Administrators

Another application of the idea of change as a fractal is to think about why some people feel they "fit" a job, department, or they district, and why sometimes they feel they just do not, no matter what happens. Some leaders are able to create change in an organization, and others cannot. Yet the same person could work with a different organization and be successful.

A leader comes to an organization and fits the culture, the pattern of the organization. The person reflects the ideas, beliefs, behaviors, and philosophy of the group or at least is close enough to be seen as similar. If that occurs, the leader may bring in a new idea, a "strange attractor" that draws energy and creates new systems within the organization. Relationships and communication are created and used to promote and sustain the efforts.

If, however, the leader is perceived as different, as "other," the new information is resisted and ignored. Relationships are not allowed to develop. Information cannot be shared adequately, and the initiatives do not succeed. The strange attractor has been lopped off, like outliers were in old statistics classes. However, the same person in a different organization may be perceived as a fit, and the efforts will be successful.

Leadership Skills Necessary to Facilitate Change

Even though change is a "journey, not a blueprint" (Fullan, 1993), there are some significant talents that a leader must use.

First, a leader must be *humble*, meaning that a leader must understand personal skills in a manner that is not boastful but comes from a position of strength. In *Good to Great* (2001), Collins describes leaders who took their companies from being good to great as persons who were more "plow horse than show horse." The leader is not necessarily the person always on stage or always in charge. Instead, the person has the humility to assess the big picture and the skills necessary in a realistic, humble fashion to facilitate movement toward the goal in a manner that is supportive of the people in the organization.

Two, a leader must *give up control*. In all honesty, we have no control; what we have is an *illusion*. The more we try to grasp something—happiness, power, wealth, joy—the more it eludes us. The more wealth we try to acquire, the more we need. The more joy we have, the more we try to clutch it or re-create it. In *The Heart of the Buddha's Teaching*, Hanh (1998) stressed that everything is impermanent because "causes and conditions change" (p. 132). "Without impermanence, life could not be. Without impermanence, oppressive political regimes would never change" (p. 132). What makes us suffer is the misguided desire to want things to be permanent when that cannot ever be. So even the good changes that occur, as well as good things that we do, will eventually be different. A leader can facilitate a process, ideas, or change, but the leader cannot *be* the process, idea, or change.

Three, a leader helps *define the issue*. By using the gifts of experience and wisdom, a leader can help define and clarify an issue.

One important tool is the ability to define the issue as a problem or dilemma. Cuban's (2001) language of problem versus dilemma is similar to Garmston and Wellman's (1999) idea of "tame and wicked problems" (pp. 221–223). A problem or "tame" problem is an issue that begs for a solution. It has an answer. A dilemma or "wicked" issue is one that cannot be solved but instead must be managed. Too often, we define issues as problems when in fact they are dilemmas. We try to "solve" dilemmas when, because of their chaotic nature, there is no simple solution.

Characteristics of a problem are as follows: (a) it begs for a solution, and (b) when the "solution" is applied, the problem disappears. For example, when buses arrive late because they cannot complete their route on time, one can change the pickup times or the school start times. Then the buses arrive on time. Another example is that when a student complains that the sun is in his eyes every day, the teacher can either move his desk or appoint him to pull the shades in the morning.

In contrast, dilemmas are issues that are "ill-defined, ambiguous, complicated, interconnected situations packed with potential conflict" (Cuban, 2001, p. 10). In addition, they "require undesirable choices between competing, highly prized values that cannot be simultaneously or fully satisfied" (Cuban, 2001, p. 10). A dilemma is complicated and must be managed, not solved. There are competing values, many times of equal weight, that beg for a compromise or something that we must "satisfice" (Cuban, 2001, p. 12), which means that to satisfy, we must often sacrifice.

Most issues in schools are dilemmas, but we treat them as problems, therefore leaving people frustrated and unwilling to continue making efforts to find resolutions to issues. However, if we correctly define the problem, we help people understand the depth of the issue.

Let's use the example of a little girl, Becky, who is disruptive in the classroom. She talks to her neighbor a lot. She passes notes. She's out of her seat a great deal. When the teacher tells her to be quiet or to get to work, she may be compliant for a little while but is shortly back to off-task behavior. The teacher tells her to sit down again. Becky acquiesces for a while, but the teacher has to remind her again the next day. The teacher may increase the consequence by having Becky stay in from recess or stay after school. When it continues, the teacher may call home, which changes the behavior for a while, but it still returns. The teacher keeps increasing the severity of the consequence—in her mind—but Becky's behavior does not really change.

The teacher has defined Becky's behavior as a problem. She has used traditional, cause-and-effect methods to try to change the behavior, but the change does not last. She believes that there is a solution to the problem if only Becky would conform. Becky believes that everything would be okay if only the teacher would not yell at her so much.

The first clue to the teacher that Becky's attention-seeking behavior is not a problem but a dilemma is when the behavior does not change with the normal interventions. In fact, it does not change when the consequences increase, particularly when Becky loses recess, her favorite part of the day. If a problem keeps returning and maybe even getting worse, it is time to redefine the issue.

If we look at Becky's behavior as a dilemma, as something that must be managed, then we must go beyond surface behaviors or words. In Becky's case, what is obvious is her misbehavior. What is not obvious is what is causing it. I believe, as do most teachers, that most students like doing the right thing, unless there are other issues. The first approach to Becky would be for the teacher to have had a one-on-one conversation with Becky to get to know her a little better and to ask a few questions. What if Becky is lonely? Sick? Afraid she is dumb? Worried about someone in her family who is ill? Has a learning disability and cannot do the work? Anyone who has ever taught knows there are a myriad reasons for behavior. We cannot deal with it effectively unless we understand what is causing it.

Let's say that Becky is disruptive because she is worried about her mother, who is sick. Treating Becky as though her behavior is the problem and then applying discipline will therefore not resolve the issue because it will not decrease the worry. It may take the stronger intervention of having Becky talk to a school nurse, getting the parents involved, providing some way for Becky to talk, and then being a little more understanding in the classroom. It may mean working with Becky to discuss some sort of plan where Becky can take a time-out if she feels too anxious or giving her 5 more minutes on the playground or connecting her with a peer mentor from the high school.

If an issue keeps recurring, then it is time to look for a deeper understanding to define the issue as a dilemma—and, therefore, chaotic—and establish a number of ways that the problem can be managed, or "satisficed." Attendance policies are a good example. There is no such thing as a perfect attendance policy. Having the "right" rules and enforcing them very strictly will not make students come to school. Why? Attendance, or lack of it, is a dilemma, not a problem. It, therefore, cannot be solved by a simple solution of stricter penalties or different consequences. In fact, all one can hope for is that it can be managed. Various groups must be "satisficed" because there is no easy solution.

Four, a leader helps determine the *real issue*. A leader must not only understand the difference between problem and dilemma but also know when the real issue is being brought forward. In education, we rush to generate possible solutions before the real issue is truly presented.

For example, recently we had a task force formed to look at how we conference with parents. Within the first 10 minutes, teachers were generating possible "solutions"—having two conferences a year and two report cards, using only portfolios, and allowing each site to choose. The list went on. The issue was not about timing and types of reporting. Instead, the issue was to look at how teachers were conferencing, whether they were conveying information or just repeating the report card. Because teachers do not receive training in conferencing and sometimes are defensive around parents, they wanted to "solve" the mechanical part of conferencing in numbers of conferences when, in fact, the issue was much larger. We needed to examine questions, such as, What type of information is necessary for parents during a conference? How much information do parents need? What is the best way of conferencing? What feedback had we gathered from parents? From students?

Eventually, we "satisficed" the group to try a combination of ideas, but it was apparent that members of the group wanted to rush to a solution so they could be finished. If we had not spent time exploring the deep issue, we would have been back right where we started—only worse—next year.

When we rush to apply simplistic solutions to complex dilemmas, we create skepticism and "silo-vision" among teaching staff. Because the issue recurs, people say we have tried this before and it did not work, so we will not bother trying again. This leads to a TTSP (this too shall pass) mentality that makes a staff reluctant to try any new idea.

Five, a leader helps *describe the metacognitive tools* for staff. An important discussion for people to have is about the definition of *problem* versus *dilemma*. If people understand the chaotic nature of dilemmas, they relax and develop management strategies. It relieves the burden of having to "solve" the issue. In meetings, it is helpful for leaders to get the group to understand the "real" issue, not just the presenting issue. Being a leader is about sharing knowledge and process so that a richer, more productive system is created.

Six, leaders are supposed to have *vision*, whatever that is. The leader may not create the vision alone, necessarily, but may create the opportunity for others to enter into the visioning process. What the leader may be able to do is to put shape around amorphous ideas of others so that a common vision begins to form. If the organization and the leader "fit," then the vision is more likely to be reflective of the larger group. If they do not fit, however, the vision is more likely to be a stand-alone idea that has little impact on the organization.

The leader may ask the group to brainstorm words that reflect their vision, then help shape the sentence(s), asking for volunteers to be on a wordsmith committee, dispersing information to groups to get feedback, and then coming back with a finished product. Gone are the days when the "leader" establishes a vision in the office and then sends it out to all parties and says, "Voila! Here is *our* vision." People need to have a voice, and leaders need to provide opportunities for voices to be heard.

Seven, a leader must be *flexible*. For example, a principal may have an idea that is presented to the district committee about the direction of professional development. The district committee listens to the idea and modifies it somewhat. The result is a better product because others have contributed with ideas the principal did not have. But if the principal had been adamant and rigid about the direction, without getting input, then a power struggle could have been the result. Then no one wins.

Eight, *listen*. Listen with your ears and your heart. So much has been written about listening, but the ability to do so effectively is the ability to listen beyond the words to hear what is truly meant. To do this, a leader must be self-aware and tuned in to the culture of the surroundings. What are the underlying issues that people are not talking about? The ability to listen is the ability to *understand*, meaning *to stand under*, and go beneath to get at the real meaning.

Nine, *it is not about you*. A leader is a facilitator. Leading is not about your needs, desires, or wishes. You are an implement, a catalyst for change. If you start getting too involved in a desired outcome, you need to step back because then it has become more about you than about the issue or the organization. You are a *means* to an end—you are not the end in itself.

SUMMARY

One must be aware of the chaotic nature of change and organizations. It is important to remember the two elements—information and relationships—that are necessary for true, lasting change to happen.

If you feel you do not "fit" the organization, then you can either listen more closely or try to adapt your strategies to more closely reflect the organization; otherwise, you may have to leave.

It is important to remember the following ideas in dealing with complex efforts:

1. It is important to view change and organizations as three-dimensional systems.

2. It is important to pay attention to the inherent paradoxes of change and organizations.

3. Change is nonlinear and can be precipitated by outliers.

4. Change is dynamic and not an end result.

5. Information and relationships are the essential components to change efforts.

6. The concept of fractals can help us understand that which previously we could not.

7. The smallest change looks like the largest.

8. Leadership skills necessary to make change happen and to be able to lead are as follows:

   Be humble

   Give up control

   Help define the issue—is it problem or dilemma?

   Help establish a joint vision

   Help describe the real issue

   Describe the metacognitive tools

   Be flexible

   Listen

   It is *not* about you

Box 2.1   Journal

1. What are some ideas about change that I can use with my staff?

2. How will I rethink some of my change initiatives?

3. When have I defined a problem as a dilemma? What was the result?

4. Other ideas. . . .

C H A P T E R   T H R E E

Positions, Like Shoes, Need to Fit

It is important to understand the need for "fit" between the strengths of the leader and the organization itself. Whether administrators are new or experienced, coming from within education or not, it is important that they do a self-assessment and then compare that to the needs of the organization.

LEADERSHIP STYLE

Michael Fullan (2001), in *The New Meaning of Educational Change*, says that effective educational leaders are "key for better or for worse" (p. 146). He reflected that two styles of leadership "that negatively affected climate, and in turn performance, were coercive (people resent and resist) and pacesetting (people get overwhelmed and burnt out)" (p. 149). So what are the attributes of an effective, positive leader?

The attributes of such as person for today's schools are those who

- value differences of opinion and even dissent,
- reculture schools and tell a new story,
- combine different leadership characteristics depending on the phase of the change process or on circumstances over time,
- are energy creators (Brighouse & Woods, 1999, p. 84),
- have qualities that cannot be captured in a checklist.

37

If attributes of a good leader could be summed up in one word, it would be *paradox* and are described as follows:

- Within a good leader is someone who can inspire followership.
- Within the power of leadership is the recognition that the more "power" one gives away, the more one has. The counterpart is that the more someone tries to grasp and hold on to power, the more elusive it becomes.
- Because the seeds of the future were sown in the past, the more a leader drives to move forward, the more he or she has to pay attention to the past.
- A leader needs to be open to change and yet willing to hold the line. Too often, educators adopt the next best thing without integrating effective practices that have worked in the past.
- A leader must be a lifelong learner who maintains a healthy skepticism and a healthy openness at the same time.
- A leader acknowledges that within mistakes are the lessons for improvement. The ability to embrace and learn from mistakes implies resiliency, a key attribute of longevity and success in the position. A principal is expected to be a manager who runs a school with clean bathrooms and enough ketchup in the lunchroom, as well as an instructional leader who facilitates the new demands of accountability and incorporation of standards to keep the school out of the newspaper for failure to make adequate yearly progress. Such tension between roles creates many possibilities for mistakes. Fullan (2001) describes that as "the worst of both worlds" (p. 138).

A common visual, the yin/yang symbol, represents that idea. Contained are the dark and the light, both of the same shape and size, opposite defenses or direction. In lightness, there is a seed of darkness; in darkness, the seed of lightness.

Just so are the lessons for improvement embedded in mistakes of the past. The key is to pay attention to those seeds. In *The Heart of the Buddha's Teaching,* Thich Nhat Hanh (1998) describes the practice of right mindfulness, meaning the ability to "bring us back to the present moment" (p. 64). That is what mistakes do—they bring us back to the present moment so that we may learn, make corrections, and move forward. Because if we do not take the opportunity to reflect on what happened, we will continue to make the same mistake over and over again.

- A leader knows that within reflection and introspection is the potential for new, outer growth. A reflective practitioner is one who looks at the side of education that is spiritual, soul-like, deep in the richness of humanity. Parker Palmer (1998), author of *Courage to Teach*, has many books and workshops relating to the task of becoming reflective with the goal of creating more effective educators.

- Another attribute of an effective leader is recognizing the moral and ethic responsibility of being an educator. Fullan (1993) said it well: "It is time we realized that teachers [and administrators] above all are moral change agents in society—a role that must be pursued explicitly and aggressively" (p. 14). Because administrators are at an even more concentrated position of power, their role as a "moral change agent" is distilled into a vital force for public education today.

How do the attributes of a leader manifest themselves into the person called a leader? Imagine a leader as walking. Sometimes leaders are out in front setting the pace, sometimes they are walking behind and reinforcing what others ahead are doing, and sometimes they walk alongside in accord with the members of the organization.

A leader who is out in front is one who may find it necessary to take people places they had not thought about going. Administrators, by virtue of their position, have an opportunity to see the larger picture of the organization. They are able to see the interaction of the local community with the community at large. They are able to be a part of the political climate and, it is hoped, influence how legislative actions affect the system. Because they have this grander view, sometimes they have to take the lead and say, "We need to look at. . . ."

Sometimes a leader has to walk behind and provide support and give gentle pushes to move forward, particularly for those who are the "late adopters" and "laggards," as defined by Jenny Rogers (2001).

People who adopt innovations fall into the following five categories: innovators (the top 2.5%), early adopters (the next 13.5%), the early majority (the next 34%), the late majority (the next 34%), and the final 16%, composing a group labeled laggards. Most of the late adopters will move forward when the major flaws have been corrected or when peer pressure is sufficient. Sometimes, the laggards just hang onto what they have always done.

For example, a certain social studies teacher enjoyed using worksheets because students used their books and worked during class time, therefore creating quiet time for the teacher. The difficulty was that the worksheets were for the textbooks *two* curriculum adoptions prior to the current book. The teacher kept a set of the really old books in his class so that students could do the worksheets. However, much of the information did not coincide with the new book or with current best practice on how history should be taught and who should be included as part of U.S. history.

Therefore, the administrator would have to push from behind by insisting that the old books leave and the well-worn masters for the worksheets be recycled. Needless to say, the teacher was highly resistant to this change.

Sometimes, a leader must lead by walking alongside. Martin Luther King Jr. took part in the freedom marches, putting himself in the same jeopardy as other marchers. A leader provides support as others come with ideas. The leader clears the path for the idea. The leader somehow provides time, financial resources, and support to clear the way for the idea.

Sometimes it is necessary to be in front, sometimes one must be alongside, and sometimes one must give a nudge. The trick to leadership is to know when to do what. Experience, good mentors, and reflective practice help a leader decide.

Assessment of an Organization's Culture

After doing a personal assessment, it is time to look at the culture of the organization where one may, or may not, apply for a position or already work currently. Success in a position is a marriage between personal skills and organizational culture. We too often think that we can be successful in any organization, and we charge ahead blindly, only to discover that the position is not a "fit."

An organization's culture is composed of so many elements, both overt and covert, that it is difficult to give a definitive description. In *Implementing Change: Patterns, Principles, and Potholes,* Gene E. Hall and Shirley M. Hord (2001) describe culture as "the individually and socially constructed values, norms, and beliefs about an organization and how it should behave that can be measured only by observation of the setting using qualitative methods" (p. 194).

Research shows that schools that have consistent leadership do well in making academic progress. We know that it takes three to five years to have a change effort at the elementary level become enculturated, five to seven years at the middle level, and seven to ten years at the high school level. Administrators who have a tendency to move on after a few years will leave a culture that is resistant to any new efforts by a new administrator because staff realize that they will outlast the administrator. Teaching staff may adopt a wait-and-see attitude. They know that if they are patient, this initiative too will pass away. Nor are they as likely to invest time and energy in developing a relationship that will be severed in a short time.

Is the Culture That of a Healthy Organization?

Organizations, like people, can be healthy or unhealthy. It is very difficult to be a healthy administrator in an unhealthy culture. One has to decide whether to take that journey.

It is probably relatively safe to say that we would all like to be healthy individuals and work in healthy organizations. Individuals work personally toward their own growth and wellness, but how does one assess the health of a large organization?

According to Richard Boyum (n.d.) of the University of Wisconsin, Eau Claire, people in a healthy organization have the following characteristics:

- Respect each other
- Care about each other
- Have reasonable knowledge of each other
- Know who is responsible for what
- Are gentle with each other
- Trust each other to tell the truth
- Are willing to share thoughts and feelings
- Meet together for good purpose
- Really listen to each other and pay attention
- Value the roles each member plays
- Where there is conflict, it is "care-fronted" more than "con-fronted"
- Allow for individuals without "title" to be leaders
- Can articulate the group's core values and goals
- Have an understanding that goals are measurable, attainable, and time bound

- Know and value that each person has a life away from the organization
- Keep a healthy balance between work and nonwork life
- Learn from the past, plan for the future, but focus on the daily priorities and responsibilities
- Celebrate success and recognize tasks "well done" on a regular basis
- Are open to change and the creative process but honor routine (i.e., things often keep working for a good reason)
- Keep learning
- Enjoy humor and laughter

An unhealthy organization is more than just the opposite of the above characteristics. It is reminiscent of the Supreme Court definition of pornography—you know it when you see it and, even more, you know it when you live in it.

An unhealthy organization does not

- Respect its members or honor their opinions and expertise
- Welcome outsiders and their differing view points
- Embrace change
- Look at itself objectively
- Accept responsibility, always offering excuses and rationales for its behavior and blaming others or organizations
- Build collegial relationships with many constituent groups

Jennifer James, an urban cultural anthropologist, professor at the University of Washington Medical School, and author of *Thinking in the Future Tense* (1996), stated, "Businesses [schools] that mistakenly assume the future will be no different from the past usually think that way because of nostalgia. The outcome can be deadly" (p. 130). She calls this trait of organization "lodges" whose

bonding power often exceeds loyalty to family or country because they create intimacy through shared ideals and beliefs, ceremonies, stories, and legends, and depend on it for their survival. The message is clear: Don't question what we're doing. Just appreciate how long we've been doing it. (p. 130)

Lodge mentality is not indicative of a healthy organization.

Types of Organizations

There are three types of organizations:

1. An organization that is unhealthy, but may not know it, but stays closed and resists making any change. The second law of thermodynamics, although designed to be descriptive of the sciences, applies to such systems. The second law states that if "no energy enters or leaves the system, the potential energy of the state will always be less than that of the initial state," which is commonly referred to as *entropy* ("Second Law," n.d.). Entropy is a measure of disorder. Basically, that means that a closed system tends to stay that way or even degenerate into more disorder as energy breaks down and is not replaced.

Unhealthy organizations, like unhealthy people, may like what is happening, for whatever reason. They are comfortable and like doing what is familiar. They believe that they can continue to do what has always been done because it has worked in the past. However, what has worked in the past may not continue to do so, and the organization may actually degenerate.

With the current access to technology and information in the United States, it is impossible to stay in one place. The paradox is that as a system resists change, eventually change will be done *to* it, instead of *with* it.

A new administrator would have many things to overcome to move an organization that is in entropy. Administrators who are personally not self-assured and healthy may buy into the system.

However, to turn it around would take a very healthy, patient person. The leader may have to be satisfied with small gains and may have to realize that the system will not change drastically unless there is an event or strong motivation to do so. In terms of the previous chapter on change, it may take the flap of a butterfly wing to create an outlier to generate energy toward a new pattern. For some organizations, that outlier may be a new administrator, or it could be loss of funding, change in superintendents or school boards, or declining enrollment. The event may have to attract energy that creates new thinking and a new way of approaching the system.

Ironically, perceived success is one of the strongest resistors to making change. Why fix something that is not broken? Collins (2001) describes that as "good is the enemy of great" (p. 1). What worked to achieve academic success in the 1960s and 1970s will not necessarily achieve academic success for all students in the 21st century.

2. An organization that is unhealthy and wants to change. This organization may recognize that it is not where it should be. In this case, an administrator has an opportunity to make changes but must understand all the stages of change—denial, anger, bargaining, depression, and acceptance. The leader must understand the time involved and not expect rapid, overnight results. There will be resistance from those who like it the way it is. This administrator would need to be self-aware, willing to be lonely, and willing to make a conscious decision about the style of change leadership to use.

A change leader, in either case of an unhealthy organization, must be able to understand the culture of the organization, both the overt and covert elements. At times, the leader will have to describe what is not working; he or she will have to describe "the elephant in the middle of the living room."

However, that will not necessarily be welcome particularly by those people who are heavily invested in keeping the organization the way it was—unhealthy and closed. That elephant has been there, and a lot of people have walked around it for a long time. Pointing it out also points out the denial in the organization. People embedded this culture will put up defenses to explain away the message. They will deny, blame others, scapegoat, and so on, all to avoid accepting responsibility.

Therefore, the leader must decide what strategy to use. In the first strategy, a Type 1 leader moves in, "picks the scab and lets the pus flow," and then moves on quickly. There is a definite place for this type of leader, a "ruffler-of-feathers," a describer of the elephant who can arouse the passion of the teachers and community to describe what is happening. This is particularly helpful if the system has been moribund.

The Type 1 leader comes in and quickly begins making assessments of the needs of the organization and starts implementing changes immediately. During the first year, this leader begins a significant change, signaling to the organization that things will not be the same from here on. This style may be useful in particularly unhealthy organizations because the leader precipitates the crisis and causes the outlier (see Chapter 2).

This leader can absorb the blame and be the scapegoat so that the administrator who follows can implement the strategies and soothe the system and look like a hero. It is difficult to be this disrupter unless one is self-aware and secure and willing to be lonely. It is difficult as a leader to be both the disrupter and someone who sees the change through unless one is willing to spend time—5 to 7 years—in the same position.

In the second strategy, a Type 2 change leader is able to move in, "pick the scab," and stay to watch the healing. This person should plan to stay no less than 5 to 7 years to work through all the stages of change/grief.

This leader will work to build relationships first and do the change second. During the first year, the Type 2 leader will not make any major changes. He or she may modify something small to signal a difference, but major changes will wait until Year 2. The first year is spent listening and building connections. By Year 2, when the leader institutes changes, the efforts will have more buy-in from many groups because of the relationships that have been developed.

The Type 2 leader is patient and willing to stay for the long journey. This person must be very self-aware and have support systems outside the organization that understand the difficulty of this task. The Type 2 leader may not be as able to understand culture and hidden issues as quickly as the Type 1 leader and therefore spends more time building relationships. Some people have the skill to see the efforts through, and some people do not. Some have the skills to disrupt, and some have the skills to soothe.

How long a person plans to stay may help determine the strategy. In education, we expect change to happen quickly, but organizations, particularly unhealthy ones, do not change very rapidly, if at all. Therefore, as one assesses a culture and whether to apply for a position, one needs to consider the health of the organization and whether one has the skills to disrupt, to disrupt and heal, or maybe neither. If one's skill is not in precipitating major reflective changes, then the candidate needs to look for healthier organizations.

3. A healthy organization. Some organizations are healthy because they work toward that goal consciously, and some are healthy because it is embedded in the culture. It takes healthy, self-aware, and self-reflective leaders and staff to maintain the health and well-being of an organization.

Fit

What does it mean to *fit* an organization? Fit is about the interaction of personal attributes and the organizational culture. Although fit is a delicate interplay among all of the items discussed here, administrators, both experienced and new, must examine the answers to the preceding question to see if they are good for the position and the position is a good fit.

FIRST SIX MONTHS

"Congratulations! We'd like to offer you the position" are sweet words to an applicant. After all the work and soul searching, now is the time and important task of putting everything together—all the hopes, training, experience, education, and excitement of the candidate with the needs and hopes of the organization.

The first six months are very telling. James (1996) talks about a culture of an organization from an insider's and outsider's perspective. James believes that outsiders have a unique opportunity to look at the culture with a fresh perspective and can, therefore, make decisions on the real issues and about how they will fit—or not. Fresh eyes see the culture from the perspective of someone who is not a part of it.

Insiders know the hidden rules, and outsiders do not. Insiders understand the power structure—who has formal power and who has informal power. Principals' secretaries often have a reservoir of informal power. Insiders understand how to access either or both.

Insiders know the stories of the organization, which are very revealing. By knowing the stories, one understands the history and understands what the organization truly values. What are the stories about? Who was involved? Who tells the stories? Who is the bearer of the culture? Who is left out?

If a person has come up through the ranks of that district to fill an administrative position, the person is an insider in the role of teacher but an outsider in the role of administrator. The new administrator may therefore have a mistaken perception of how quickly change can be effected.

It is different if one comes in from the outside. During the first six months, it is important to learn about the culture. Listen carefully to conversations in the hallway, in staff meetings, and in the lounge. Use this time to gather more information about personal fit in the organization. If one "fits," then it is fun to put background, needs, and culture together to enjoy the position and work hard to make a difference. James (1996) believes that once a person has been in an organization or position for 6 months, then that person then becomes part of the system and is less likely to be able to describe the culture objectively. After a person has been in a system for two years, he or she has *become* the system.

Therefore, if an applicant is brought in to be a change agent, there is a small window of opportunity to make changes. And as described above, if the applicant is meant to be a Type 1 change agent and then move on, he or she needs to make changes within the first two years. If this person wants to be a Type 2 change agent because he or she wants to remain in the system, then this person is most effective in building relationships, making no major changes the first year, listening to the voices of the organization, making changes the second year, and modifying the efforts for at least the next three to five years.

If, however, the position does not feel like a fit, then the reflective practitioner can make conscious choices about next steps. The person can work hard for three years and gain experience to move to the next opportunity. He or she can learn as much as possible, network with others, and build a résumé that will help this person reach an ultimate career goal.

SUMMARY

The ability to lead is a complex interplay among the leader, the community, the district, and the skills of all of the above. There is a difference between healthy and unhealthy organizations, and sometimes even a healthy leader cannot change an organization that does not want to move. These are difficult decisions because the leader often takes it personally. But once again, the chaotic interaction of the three-dimensional system allows change to happen. If there is a definite match between expectations of the organization and skills of the leader, then the administrator can look forward to a difficult job, but one that will make a difference.

In contrast, if it feels like it does not fit, the administrator has some choices to make. Leaving the organization or staying long enough to see changes occur are two possibilities. Too many frequent moves on a résumé are a red flag to human resource offices.

Plus, there is something to be learned from any position. Staying on a job for three years and then moving on to gain more skills is not uncommon. There is always something to learn, even in a situation that is less than perfect, so use the time to expand your repertoire.

When, however, a person finds an organization that feels good, use the time to continue to learn and grow. Take the time to be a reflective practitioner who models what it means to be a moral, ethical leader.

Box 3.1   Journal

1. Are my skills a fit for the organization I am working in?

2. Would I characterize my organization as healthy or not? Why? Am I able to effect change?

3. What was an "aha" about healthy or unhealthy organizations and "fit"?

4. What "mistakes" have I made that have been valuable learning experiences?

C H A P T E R   F O U R

Learning the New Rules of Communication

Becoming an administrator necessitates a change in communication patterns. There are distinct communication groups—building administrators, teachers, noncertified staff, and district office staff—each with its own rules. Communication between groups and within a group depends on a person's peer group. The amount of perceived power of the group and the number of members within the group help shape communication styles. When some people change peer groups, particularly by moving up the hierarchy from teacher to administrator, a new set of communication patterns is necessary.

COMMUNICATION BETWEEN GROUPS

According to the work of David Tyack and Myra Strober (1981), authors of a paper prepared for the National Institute of Education on the history of sexual structuring in educational employment, American schools were created as a reflection of the family system in practice at the time. The father, head of the family, was in charge. Power and authority rested in that position and was dispersed only at the whim and beneficence, or lack thereof, of the male in charge. There was a hierarchy: father, father and mother, and children. Power dissipated as it traveled downward.

49

The same hierarchy is replicated in our school system, both at the district level and within a building. At the macro level, the superintendent is in the seat of authority. At the micro level, the head principal is in charge, with power filtering through assistants. At the micro-micro level, teachers are in charge of their classrooms, and students have the least power and control. The system is like a hologram in that each subset looks like the whole. A teacher within a classroom has the same bureaucratic system as the superintendent within a district. The hierarchical and segmented structure of our system has created a series of in-groups and out-groups. The different subgroups are visible by their different labor bargaining units. Paraprofessionals, custodians, food service workers, teachers, clerical staff, administrators, superintendents, and school board groups constitute some of the subgroups. When groups are in competition with one another for remuneration, automatic barriers in communication and trust are created because within the culture, the person who makes the most money has the most power and prestige. This is true at the macro and micro levels. Therefore, communication becomes inhibited due to the unequal pay structure, which is theoretically based on levels of responsibilities and difficulties of the job. However, that does not stop the problems of jealousy, resentment, and barriers.

Communication patterns among groups reflect these differences. Within a group, communication occurs relatively equally between peers. Communication and socialization are more likely to be open and honest within a group than between groups. Because formal power is relatively equal, communication can be more equal. (We know that within any group, there are informal power structures as well.)

Communication either down or up the hierarchy, however, is less likely to be completely open. Going down the ladder of prestige—as from teacher to custodian or from administrator to teacher—communication is likely to be in the form of directives. Teachers may tell custodians, "Please clean my room every day, not every other." Administrators tell teachers what to do. "We ask that teachers stand outside their door between classes." Superintendents will tell principals that they must submit budget requests by April 1. Personal communication going down the hierarchy around areas such as family, hobbies, or interests is relatively limited. It may happen that two people discover a commonality, such as golfing, but even then the relationship tends to be superficial.

Likewise, if communication goes up the hierarchy, it is likely to be more guarded because of the power differential. It is often requesting something—information, money, or time. People lower in the hierarchy do not want to make themselves vulnerable. Teachers are not likely to be completely honest with their principals about their fears of professional inadequacy, for example. They may share with a peer, but not a superior.

Principals are not likely to be completely open with the superintendent about everything that occurs within a building for fear of being seen as weak or incompetent. Each person decides just how open to be with superiors. This is one reason peer group support is so important, so that peers can ask questions of each other to help problem solve without the fear of judgment.

Communication among groups in schools is a common focus of improvement in almost any strategic plan. The communication bottleneck is created by our hierarchical structure. Those groups farther down in the hierarchy often say they do not know what is going on. Teachers say that directives come down from the top but that there is little real communication with true sharing of ideas. Administrators talk *at* them but do not listen or share ideas.

The compartmentalized daily task of teaching exacerbates the problem. Elementary teachers spend their day in the classroom with "their" students. They often socialize professionally and personally, particularly along grade-level lines. Fifth-grade teachers may meet and share ideas. First-grade teachers may plan parties together.

High school teachers spend the day teaching their 150 students in *their* room. They often socialize along departmental lines or with near-physical neighbors. Meetings are held for departments. Math teachers meet to decide sectioning. But math teachers seldom meet with art teachers to socialize unless there is close physical proximity or shared lunch assignments that force people to get to know one another.

Changes

One of the biggest losses a new administrator feels is the change in friendships with teachers who were former peers but are now subordinates. New ground rules must be established as to which are appropriate topics of conversation and which are not.

Teachers often share complaints about administration. When one is promoted, particularly within the same system, it is no longer possible to take part in this discussion. Another difficulty is that, as an administrator, one is privy to confidential information. When teacher-friends have complaints and concerns, administrators cannot always share what they know. Some friends may resent the fact that communication patterns have changed. They may resent that the former friend, now an administrator, knows more and cannot or will not share information. Some friendships may not survive this change in power differential. It takes a true friend to be able to work through the changes in boundaries.

Even casual friendships change when a person becomes an administrator, especially if the promotion occurs within the same system. For example, in one situation, an administrator was part of a book club whose members were all teachers. Conversations during the evening would stray to discussing school. People would vent and then ask the administrator for her understanding of the issue. However, that knowledge was not public data. Over time, the administrator had to phase out of membership in the club.

It is easier to maintain friendships with teacher-friends if one changes districts because appropriate boundaries between professional and personal can remain. Teachers can discuss administrators without there being a conflict of interest.

As one principal described it, "When the rest of my colleagues as teachers were developing social relationships and friendship teams, I was already a principal so that those networks and teams are more limited" (Sigford, 1995, p. 132).

Communications About *the District*

In the macro system, building administrators are middle management, the persons responsible for delivering district messages in support of district initiatives. In the micro system of a building, assistant principals are expected to support and promote publicly the decisions of the principal, even if they disagree personally. Both expectations reflect the hierarchy of the early American family. Both parents present a unified front to the children, even if they disagree between themselves.

Each professional owes a certain respect and allegiance to the institution that signs the paycheck. Yet each person, individually, owes the same respect to personal values. If there is conflict between the two, the professional must decide how to deal with it.

One choice is to leave and work for another district. Another is to agree, no matter what. Another is to rebel and be prepared for the consequences. Still another is to practice "creative insubordination." For example, if there is a district decision to become involved in a certain staff development project districtwide and the principal knows that this is not valuable or timely, the principal may choose to be the last on the list of schools to implement this decision. By the time the initiative hits the particular school, the movement may have lost energy. Although delaying action and practicing minimal compliance are passive-aggressive, they may be necessary for survival.

Another choice is to tell only half the story. Sometimes, teachers do not need or want to know the whole story. They want the essence of the information but not all of the gory details. Teachers want administrators to take care of politics and policies so they can do what they do best—teach. Unless it affects them directly, teachers believe that a good administrator keeps the burden of politics away from them. Therefore, if teachers do not need the whole story, tell them only the parts that they need to know when they need to know them.

Communications Within the Role as Administrator

Supra-Parent

One surprising part of the role of administrator includes the part as a "supra-parent." The supra-parent role is much like the "father" in the hierarchical system. The administrator is the grand communicator of the building. Staff, students, and parents look to the administration to be the expert, the "bottom line," the problem solver, and, sometimes, the priest/priestess. It is a difficult role, one for which we receive little training.

As an assistant principal, I watched the demands placed on the head principal. Everyone wanted to have her attention and ear. They needed information from her. Furthermore, they wanted to keep her apprised of events in the building.

I watched a guidance counselor interact with her. He spent 15 minutes telling her every detail when what he really needed was five minutes to problem solve a particular detail. He told her every detail about the setup for schoolwide testing. She did not need to know each detail of the setup because she trusted him to act professionally to accomplish the task. What she really needed to know was what he needed from her.

What she needed was the "sound bite," the bottom line. On the surface, the conversation was about testing. What was underneath was his need for honoring the amount of work he was expending to make the testing happen. What he needed was a connection with the supra-parent. She needed the sound bite. His needs and her needs were conflictual; he needed time and approval, and she needed information and more time to spend with others.

His interchange with her took more than 15 minutes. In a building of 2,000 students, 120 teachers and staff, plus custodians, food service workers, parents and families, and community and district responsibilities, there are not enough 15-minute blocks of time to go around. Even if most interactions take five to seven minutes, a principal would have time for 78 single interactions throughout a school day during school hours. If each interaction took 15 minutes, there would be time for only 26 interactions—without any time for lunch. As we know, meetings, parent conferences, and other conversations may take an hour or more. It is no wonder that most administrators carry on more than one conversation at a time. It is not unusual to see an administrator on the telephone and writing a message to another person at the same time, with two people standing in line waiting their turn. There is not enough time in the day for all the interactions people would like. It is difficult to be that supra-parent.

Repetition

Another part of the grand communicator role is to realize that teachers have a tendency to repeat themselves to a fault. There is a mistaken practice that if one repeats something numerous times, it will be heard. That does not work in a family, in a classroom, or in dealing with administrators. Children, students, and administrators learn to tune out the first two or three times and pay attention only to the bottom line.

Administrators learn quickly which people to listen to, as well as which people give them unbiased information. Repeating something does not make it true or important.

Listen for the Real Message

It is necessary to learn to listen for the real message. As an administrator, one realizes that the job consists of being responsive, being effective at giving information, and, particularly, being a good listener. Being a good listener means hearing the underlying message that may be hidden in the spoken words. For example, if a teacher comes to discuss how "some" teachers are not doing their job (standing in the hall between classes), it may be that the real issue is that the next-door neighbor, who is not very likeable, is not doing supervision. The teacher wants the administrator to reprimand this person because it is not "fair" that some people do what is expected and others do not.

To get at real issues, the administrator must understand the culture of the organization, as well as the personalities involved, and make decisions about the real issue. Therefore, the administrator must decide what action to take, if any. The action taken may be different from that requested by the message giver because the administrator has to decide the real issue.

Rephrase and Reframe

An administrator must be able to listen, rephrase, and reframe. (There is more on this skill in Chapter 7.) Part of being a good listener is separating the issue from the presenter. For example, some teachers do not have the best presentation skills. They may be abrupt or gruff. When asked to patrol the halls before vacation, a teacher may fire back, "It's not my job." It is difficult not to respond quickly, "Yes, it is" instead of working with the person to understand the big picture of how everyone must help on intense days. But it is not easy to divorce communication styles from the message.

Administrators are victims of constant negative comments, complaints, and interactions. Comments in the staff lounge, such as, "That's why they make the big bucks," for example, are partly true in that it is the task of administrators to be responsible and problem solvers. But teachers do not understand how much of an administrator's day is spent resolving problems.

It is doubly important to hear the real issue. When a person is frustrated or upset, what come out first are surface emotions. The real emotions come out later. For example, a parent on the telephone is angry that a teacher has not communicated on a regular basis when the student was not doing well in class. However, after further conversation, the administrator understands that the parent is blaming the school for what is really an issue between parent and child. The child is not doing well, and the parent would rather blame the school than deal with the child and with the child-parent relationship. It is always easier to blame someone else than to look in the mirror—not necessarily productive, but often easier. However, it takes time to listen and help reshape the conversation to discuss what is really helpful to the parent.

Whose Issue Is It?

What is difficult for an administrator is to decide whose issue it is. Everyone feels like they have a certain impunity in "dumping" issues on an administrator. "Just wanted you to know. . . ." However, the "dumpee" drops the issue in the office and walks out feeling relieved, but the administrator must decide how much of the issue to take on. Whose issue is it? Administrators do not have the luxury of "dumping back."

For example, one day a probationary teacher was inappropriate with students. The teacher wanted a student suspended because of a power struggle with the student. However, the teacher had inappropriately precipitated the struggle. It was inappropriate to suspend the student for the adult's bad behavior. The teacher accused the administrator of not doing the job. However, the teacher needed to understand that part of the problem belonged to the teacher— the adult. Administrators want to be supportive of teachers, but students are sometimes held hostage in the middle because of adult bad behavior, which makes it doubly important to discover the real issue.

People are mistaken when they believe that administrators are at the top of the hierarchy, because when it comes to negativity this hierarchy is inverted. Administrators become the bottom of a very large pile, and negativity rolls downhill. Many people feel that they can say anything with impunity to an administrator and that the administrator has to take it. To a degree, that is true. Administrators are the first to hear if something is wrong and one of the last to hear if something is good.

Communication With the Larger Community

According to DuFour and Eaker (1998), when parents receive frequent and effective communication "from their children's school, their involvement increases, their overall evaluation of educators is more favorable, and their attitudes toward the school and its program improves" (p. 241).

Communication with the larger community becomes increasingly necessary in this time of instant communication. Effective principals use technology to get information to parents. One can establish electronic address books and online communications to keep constituents informed. It is important that a 21st-century administrator be facile with various means of getting the word out. We have voice mail, e-mail, fax, and snail mail for methods of communication. It is important for administrators to communicate well and frequently.

It is likewise important for administrators to coach staff to do the same. Effective communication is timely, is not excessively demanding on teachers, celebrates success as well as identifies concerns, and is two-way (DuFour & Eaker, 1998, pp. 242–243). Teachers fear that if they post all their course syllabi and grades, parents will be more demanding. Many teachers have found the opposite to be true. When parents are informed about the progress of their child, they have been more in charge of the student's work at home, and parent-teacher conferences have become more meaningful.

As parents are more informed and more educated, it is imperative to keep them informed so they can be interactive partners in the educational process.

Communication Distancing

It is difficult to experience constant negativity and not take it personally. Administrators need to establish a pattern that I call *communication distancing* to survive. One must be self-reflective and self-aware and able to separate the message from the message giver.

Part 1: Administrator as an Information Filter

Part 1 of distancing is to know when to relay everything you know and when to withhold certain information. Administrators must learn to be honest—with protection. It is important that the principals relay information from the superintendent and school board. However, because they often have information from many sources, it is necessary for administrators to act as a filter, to try to sort out fact and fiction, and to protect privacy rights of individuals. There are times when parents come to talk to the principal. For example, parents may have a concern that their child is not learning in social studies class. Parents do not see homework. The child complains that the students never get assignments turned back. However, at progress report time, the child has a failing grade. The parents complain to the principal. What the parents do not know and cannot know is that the principal is working on a corrective action plan for that teacher because the teacher is not doing the job correctly. However, the principal has to develop the communication skills of listening to the parents and letting them know that there is action being taken without defaming the teacher. Here the administrator must be honest with the parents, but not totally so.

The administrator is not withholding information, but is acting as a clearinghouse for what is appropriate. But there are some things an administrator cannot talk about because of data privacy laws, and some people just have to trust that the administrator is doing the right thing. It is important that the administrator has built successful relationships with the staff so that trust is in place.

Part 2: Knowing When Anger Is Not Really Anger

Part 2 of communication distancing involves knowing when anger that is directed at an administrator is really a part of the denial stage of the grief process. By the time someone gets to an administrator, he or she is often angry. It is important that the administrator put the anger aside to deal with the real issue. A parent comes to the office irate that his daughter has not received total cooperation with her 504 plan, which is a federal law designed to help people, including students, who have an impairment in one of life's major functions. He has been frustrated because he is not getting the support he felt necessary from teachers and counselors. By the time he gets to an administrator, he has already experienced several layers of bureaucracy and is not happy.

At this point, it may be an effective strategy is to let him vent, realizing that his words are not personal. The next step is to ask him what he would like, assuring him that both school and family want what is best for his daughter. The third step is to formulate an action plan. The fourth step is to plan a time to come back to revisit, either by telephone or in person, how things are going. The follow-up is crucial because it signals that the school is serious and wants to be involved over a period of time.

This example is too common but is typical because the anger may be symptomatic that this parent is stuck in a stage of the grief/change process as discussed in Chapter 1. When any child is born, parents have dreams and wishes for what this child will be. Those children seldom materialize. Parents of children who are not perfect or who have disabilities must go through the grief process to mourn the "loss" of the perfect child that they dreamed of. If they have not gone through the reality of grieving this loss, it is all too easy to blame the school, a teacher, or an ex-spouse. If one can understand the origins of the anger, it is easier to maintain an appropriate distance.

An excellent resource is *Dealing With Difficult Parents (and With Parents in a Difficult Situation)* by Todd Whitaker and Douglas Fiore (2001).

Part 3: Maintaining Distant Relationships in a Building

Part 3 of distancing is knowing how to maintain respectful yet distant relationships in a building. In other words, it is very difficult to be friends with people one supervises and evaluates. As a teacher, one had the opportunity to have a friendship with many teachers. As one of a very small team of administrators, one may or may not find a comrade. One must find relationships outside the building that can provide support.

Some principals who are in isolated areas said they maintained contacts with friends who live in different communities. One said that she used to "call my friends, cry, and have a big phone bill" (Sigford, 1995).

Generally, it is not a good idea to become a close personal friend with someone within the building. The power and information differential causes too many awkward situations. There are things that teachers cannot know. Anyone who has worked in a school knows how fast the gossip network works among staff. It is an oxymoron to "share a secret." The temptation the other person has to just tell one person, share one little piece, is just too tempting when we work in a people business. Therefore, an administrator who wants to protect privacy should not confide in anyone.

It is normal to discuss students and staff with others in our building. Information about people, whether it is about students, administrators, teachers, or parents, is a rapidly exchanged commodity. Even if an administrator shares impressions or ideas, those thoughts have a market value in the lounge because everyone wants to know about what the administrators think and do because that affects the entire school, either directly or culturally. Therefore, it is important that an administrator maintain a certain self-protective distance from persons in the building.

Because the position of administrator is lonely and there are few peers, building administrators tend to gravitate toward counselors or social workers as possible sympathetic ears. Part of the reason is that administrators and counselors/social workers are in close working proximity. The helping positions are in a unique position in a building by being on the teachers' contract but having an extended yearly contract more like that of an administrator. Teachers often see people in those roles as neither teacher nor administrator. In small systems, someone in those roles may even fill in for an administrator when an administrator is out of the building.

Counselors and social workers often have a more global perspective on the workings of a school than teachers. Therefore, counselors and administrators often find themselves more aligned physically and professionally than do administrators and teachers. Yet, a friendship with a counselor is precarious and open to criticism. An administrator is still in an evaluative position over a counselor.

Part 4: Distance Within the Administrative Ranks

Part 4 of distancing is the communication distance one experiences within the administrative ranks. Everyone needs someone to talk to; administrators are no different. Administrators are most secure in confiding in other administrators. That, too, may be problematic. If the administrative team is not cohesive, it is difficult to share with people who may be competitive on their way to the top. It may be difficult to find someone on a small team who thinks the same way.

One principal used the state principal organization to develop a support network. Another said, "The men have their fishing. We [women administrators] get together and talk. I get recharged because I have professional friends" (Sigford, 1995, p. 130).

Confiding in administrative superiors is fraught with difficulty. For an assistant principal, it may be problematic to be completely open with the principal. Principals may be reserved in what they share with superintendents, although in small districts, principals may confide in superintendents as the only peers within the system. Communications are guarded and distant, however, because of the power differential. Truly open communication rarely goes up the power ladder. One principal said, "Now it's hard to have friends at my own level. There is only 'one of me' at my level. This professional distance is hard because there are few women to relate to" (Sigford, 1995, p. 132). The scarcity of peers is even more exaggerated for administrators of color.

Because peers are difficult to access and one does not confide "up," it is not surprising that administrators often confide in their head secretaries. The administrator feels safe in sharing because there is a wide gap between the level of responsibilities for principal and secretary. Yet the secretary sees the school from a wide-angle lens, unlike the narrow focus of teachers. The secretary is there as a watchdog and as helpmate for the principal. The secretary is in a prime position to feed the administrator a lot of powerful information about the building. There is a certain protective feeling a good secretary has for an administrator. Secretaries know many personal details about the administrators because they field phone calls, visitors, and appointments.

However, it is the rare secretary who feels free to reciprocate the confidences. Secretaries may be selective in what personal information they share with the principal. The differential is evident in the fact that many head principals do not have more than a surface knowledge of the personal lives of their secretaries. Because the principal shares and feels close to the secretary, there is an assumption that the reciprocal is true, but often is not, because of the power differential.

In the days of only male principals, the head custodian was sometimes the same type of safety valve as the head secretary. The old boiler room was a place for the principal to have a cigarette, tell a few stories, and relax. But the power differential continued. A custodian could not say the same things to a principal as the principal could say to the custodian.

Part 5: Emotional Detachment

Part 5 of the distancing process is that administrators are expected to be emotionally detached from information. They are expected to be steadfast, nonemotional, concerned, and even-tempered. When angry, they are expected to control their temper. When sad, they are expected to control their tears. In fact, if administrators are too demonstrative, confidence in them may decrease.

If there is tension, anger, sadness, or other feelings in the building, the whole building is fine if the administrator is stoic and strong. If, however, the administrator is shaky, the whole building is shaky. As in a family, if the head of the family is OK, so is the rest of the family.

Unfortunately, the demonstration of feelings has been misinterpreted culturally as being weak or ineffectual. A superintendent once said, as he rated other superintendents, that the people were good superintendents because they "did not show emotion." Interesting criterion! It is not true that the demonstration of sadness, joy, anger, or happiness makes one less effective as an administrator. However, our White, male model has left us this standard. Administrators are to be involved but detached—a difficult road to walk.

Some people would say that this attitude has changed in the past few years. I disagree. The comment from the superintendent describing good candidates was made in 2004. He was not atypical.

Recognition of this hidden rule is difficult for women and for some cultures. Culturally, American women have been trained to be the emotions for a relationship and/or family. Many women interviewed for my dissertation found it difficult to curb their normal emotional responses to events. They had to confine their feelings to a very few trusted friends or spouses and demonstrate them only behind closed doors. "You can't say what you'd like to say" (Sigford, 1995, p. 130). Even with a spouse as a support person, one woman said, "Funny, because I never talk about school with him because he gets bored. But he's always there" (Sigford, 1995, p. 131). Women learn to close their doors and emote in private, maintaining a public persona of control.

A possible answer to this issue may occur as more and more women and more people of color assume leadership roles. They may be a vital force in changing the traditionally stoic image. The ability to display feelings may be a humanizing experience for some in a building, recognizing that to be human is to have emotions, particularly as we embrace different cultural styles. As the model for leadership changes with more collaboration, the image of the more stoic leader may also change.

SUGGESTIONS FOR ESTABLISHING COMMUNICATION PATTERNS

1. If something is truly a secret, do not tell anyone.

2. Develop peers outside of the building who can act as sounding boards and confidants. Such people may be found in professional organizations or be administrators in other buildings within the district or in similar positions in different systems.

3. Find a safe place within the building to regroup. This may be a place to which to escape for a few minutes, such as the office of a support person (e.g., the office of the gifted/talented coordinator), the kitchen, the choir room, or the custodian's workroom.

4. Take time. It is important to take time to think and look at an issue with a wide-lens perspective. If a teacher presents an issue, listen to the details, take notes, and then take 24 hours to think it over, if possible. We have a tendency to want to answer too quickly, before there is time to think of all the ramifications. In fact, sometimes by waiting a day, the issue will take care of itself. Do not stall to avoid a difficult issue, but use time as an ally to seek a possibly better solution. It is perfectly permissible to say, "I need to think about this. I'll get back to you tomorrow."

5. Members of staff and community expect administrators to be solid and even-tempered. Appearing flustered or upset makes people distrustful of the decisions. Therefore, it is important to hear difficult things and not get rattled. Unfortunately, this part of the culture persists.

If there is an emotional response, however, do not feel belittled. It is beneficial to staff and students alike to see someone be human. It may help change the stereotype of administrative behavior as staff and community see someone who is emotionally appropriate still be a capable administrator. It is appropriate to laugh, cry, show anger, or be frustrated in different situations. It is appropriate to show emotion, but it is not appropriate for emotions to rule the decision.

6. Repeat only the positive parts of a story. It is the task of the administrator to create a positive atmosphere in a building. This is not to suggest becoming a Pollyanna. However, positive behavior begets other positive behavior, which creates a positive culture.

7. Use experiences that were less than successful as lessons. There is no such thing as a bad mistake, only one we do not learn from. If we do not learn the first time we make a mistake, we will re-create it in some form until we get the message. As an administrator, it is our task to discover the lesson we need to learn and then frame it in a learning perspective.

8. Use technology to get the message out. It is sometimes difficult to establish the right tone in an e-mail, so if the issue is

burning, write the e-mail, let it sit for half an hour while doing something else, and then come back and read it aloud to see how it sounds. There is a certain e-mail etiquette, such as that all caps means a LOUD VOICE or SHOUTING, that we need to learn.

If the issue is somewhat sensitive, pick up the telephone. It is difficult to send nuances through e-mail, and it is easier to have a telephone conversation and relate with tone of voice. Or if it is really important, go see the person so that there can be a face-to-face conversation.

Remember, e-mails are public data. Whatever is on your computer can be accessed by others. So, if the response is supposed to be private, either call or go see the person.

9. If there is a day or time when the job is overwhelming, find an excuse to leave the building for a few minutes. Find something to take to the central office. Go to the post office. Go visit a peer to talk about a committee. Take time to put distance between the issue and you. Tomorrow is another day.

Box 4.1   Journal

1. What are my communication strengths?

2. When do I need to become more distant in my communication?

3. How can I improve the information that I send out? Do it more frequently? A more timely manner?

4. What would my staff say is my strength in the area of communication?

5. How, if any, did the communication patterns change when I became an administrator?

6. When do I use communication distancing?

7. How, if any, have I changed my communication patterns?

8. What are my strengths in communicating with the larger community?

CHAPTER FIVE

Maintaining Control of Time

F or teachers, the school day is dictated by bells and someone else's timetables. There is constant pressure to be on time, to finish the lesson before the bell rings, and to complete preparation for the next class during prep hour.

It is an assumption that administrators have more flexibility in their personal schedule because they are not as bound by bells. Plus, an administrator has a secretary to help keep a calendar, which leads to another assumption: that an administrator has control over the way time is spent during the day.

That is true only to a degree. Most educators spend more than 40 hours a week to do their job. Administrators certainly do. There are many constituents to satisfy. The day starts early and ends late because of evening commitments. There is work on weekends. One principal said it this way, "If you're a high school principal, you LIVE this job. You don't have a choice not to" (Sigford, 1995, p. 130). Elementary principals would say the same. Many come in to work on weekends when the telephone does not ring and no one needs a question answered.

Teachers have a minimum day as set by contract. We all know that most teachers spend more than that. For administrators, however, the contract is not as clear. The term *professionalism*, which is supposed to describe those "other duties as assigned," includes a wide variety of duties. Teachers have the same phrase in their contract, but as one moves up the hierarchy in a school, that description includes more demands on time. Teachers have fewer demands than assistant principals. Assistants have fewer demands than head principals. There is no such thing as enough time—for anyone.

HAVE YOU GOT A MINUTE?

It is rare that a principal has a quiet minute to reflect. If a principal is in the office, there are people at the door or on the telephone. If a principal goes out into the halls, he or she is invariably greeted with the phrase, "Have you got a minute?" which has to be the most deceptive phrase used by teachers. The minimizing of the time is a gentle way to get the attention of administrator, knowing full well that few interactions, especially business interactions, take only a few minutes. In reality, that "minute" will last any-where from five to thirty minutes. It does not take too many "Have you got a minute(s)?" to eat away the hours of the day.

The other phrase that is frequently used to get the attention of an administrator is "One quick question. . . ." The question may be quick, but the answer seldom is. If someone is asking an adminis-trator a question, then there is some confusion to be cleared up or clarification to be given. That can rarely be done by a simple sentence. Indeed, if it were that simple, the person would not have to be asking. Therefore, beware of deceptively simple questions because they beg for complicated, time-consuming answers.

For example, the secretary wants to know what to do because there are not enough substitute teachers. Classes must be covered. Another example is when food service asks how many students will be absent the next day for field trips. Maybe students come to ask how they can finance a student council retreat. A teacher wants to know what the schedule will be for the fourth-grade tests and what rooms will be affected. There are few quick questions and fewer quick answers. It is doubtful that any of the above examples can be answered by "one quick answer."

Time is one of the most precious commodities for teachers and administrators alike. Because of the constant sense of passing time, teachers are always in a rush. They know they have to be somewhere soon. If they want to talk during the five minutes between classes, they know they must be in the room ready to start when the bell rings. If they try to talk during lunch, they know that they will choke down their sandwich in five to ten minutes, run off a test, and talk to the administrator within their 25-minute slot.

Most of the time pressures for an administrator come from interactions with people. Teachers have questions, students have concerns, and parents need answers. Parents believe that schools are open to them at any time, whenever they want to drop in. They do not feel the need to make appointments as they would for doctors or lawyers. In addition, when they just drop in, it is usually because of a problem and they are, most likely, upset or angry. They get doubly angry if they cannot be seen and they are taken care of *immediately*. Because schools are public institutions, it is important to be customer-friendly. However, it is frustrating because there is a fine line between being customer-friendly and aiding and abetting inappropriate rude behavior. Although it is necessary to be responsive to parent needs, it is also appropriate to ask people to make appointments if the issue is not urgent.

It seems that interactions are largely on a demand basis. Teachers get frustrated if administrators do not provide enough lead time for such things as grade reporting or communication with parents. However, the reciprocal does not seem to hold true. There are always a few teachers who are notorious for barely or not making deadlines, such as turning in grades or getting in information for announcements. What would these teachers do if students did that to them? One wonders. . . .

In administrative offices, a closed door appears to mean nothing. In polite circles, a closed door means that privacy is requested. In our culture, it is expected that people should knock on the closed door and wait for a response, such as, "Come in," before entering. However, some teachers do not believe that a closed door means that it is closed to *them*. It is as though their individual issue is so important that polite rules can be ignored.

Are people, particularly teachers, impolite or just rude? First, teachers are constantly under a time pressure, which creates a sense of urgency for their respective issues. They want to accomplish one task and get on to the next, and they have a limited time to do that.

One example is the way teachers interrupt conversations. If two teachers or a teacher and an administrator are having a conversation, and a third person approaches with an issue, it is *extremely* rare for the third party to wait before interjecting his or her ideas, which this person thinks of as urgent. Unfortunately, people who do this are rude. They do not show respect for the conversation that was occurring when they just interrupt, disregarding the intensity or depth of the conversation that was invaded.

The primacy of their issue appears to take precedence over polite behavior. In addition, teachers will talk to a principal while the principal is having another conversation on the telephone. Although we have two ears, one for the telephone and one for the person, both ears connect to the same brain and can register only one conversation at a time. Although administrators learn to multitask, it is important to ask people to wait until one can devote one's entire attention to the conversation.

Just Say No

It is necessary to learn the skill of saying no. The presence of an administrator is a desired commodity for all events and meetings because a personal appearance shows the necessary support from the building leader. It is a component of that supra-parent role where everyone wants the person in charge to be engaged with all aspects of what happens within a school. In many ways, it is nice to be so wanted and so influential. It is not possible, however, to do it all.

Therefore, set priorities. Attend each sport once during the season. Attend one concert during the season. Set priorities as to which committees are to be a focus and then delegate responsibility. Use assistant principals, teacher leaders, and athletic directors to provide administrative presence. Sometimes, one will have to say, "No, I'm sorry, but I cannot attend."

At the elementary level, it is difficult to say no to any curriculum night or book fair. Principals may not want to do that because a lot of business happens on those nights, such as that which occurs in casual conversations with parents.

The counterpart of saying no is to make sure that one says yes to the positive parts of being an administrator. Go to recognition ceremonies when students and staff are honored for achievement. There is nothing any better.

Remember—set priorities and schedule time based on goals. No one will set these priorities for you.

Use Technology to Help With Time Pressures

Technology can help with time. Use a PDA that can synch with a secretary, so you both can have access to the calendar to make changes and see what appointments are scheduled when and where. In using a PDA, one strategy is to have the secretary use all capital letters when entering an appointment and the principal use lower case. That way, it is easy to see who scheduled the information and whom one can ask for more information.

Synch the PDA on a daily basis. Things change so quickly. Or use the calendar through the e-mail system to set up meetings on a district level.

Use shared folders and intranets to communicate with a set group of people. For example, use a shared folder to set agendas for principal meetings. Everyone can enter items and save the time of calling a secretary or contacting a particular person.

Use e-mail to send messages to several people at one time, instead of making many separate telephone calls.

One can use conference calls or calls through the Internet to talk to someone hundreds of miles away, thereby preempting the need to travel far distances to get answers.

The ways to use technology are endless. Unfortunately, it was envisioned that technology would save us time. Instead, we have more interactions and believe that the interactions should be faster. We now get junk mail four ways instead of one—by fax, e-mail, telephone, and "snail" mail. In addition, there is a time limit that is unofficially assigned to responding. People expect a response to a telephone call within 24 hours and a response to an e-mail within the day.

To manage all of the information, an administrator should come in before school and answer all telephone calls and e-mails. It is helpful to do this again at lunch and then again at the end of the day. However, a telephone call after 3:00 on a Friday afternoon, can be a problem. It is okay to wait until Monday to answer, and if one is lucky, the issue will be resolved.

Suggestions for Handling Your Day

1. Interruptions are our business. An administrator's job is to be of service to the school and community. People come for help, answers, consolation, to use one as a sounding board, and to be a friend. There are never two days that are the same; the job will never be boring. The interruptions and meetings all provide a richness and variety that most professions do not have.

2. Understand that a task will seldom be completed at one sitting. Begin to see the demands and interruptions *as* the job, instead of as distractions *from* the job. Reframing helps people realize that administrators are meant to serve others, instead of the opposite.

3. One of the best times to get things done, to clean off the desk, is the second hour after school is over. Most urgent interactions have taken place in that first hour after school. By the next hour, most people are out of the building. Most parents think that people are gone and do not try to call, or if they do call, they believe they will get voice mail.

4. A way to make good use of time is to know how to access your school computer from home. There may be times when it is more efficient to work at home for an hour, send it to yourself at work, and get the task done. An hour of uninterrupted work at home may accomplish what could not happen during three hours of interruptions at work.

5. On the other hand, it may be healthier to work hard at work and then go home and leave school in the school building. One of the fastest ways to burn out in administration or in any other job is to do it seven days a week, 24 hours a day. Everyone needs a day of rest. Administrators need two. As far as possible, do not work on weekends. Do something different on weekends so that by Monday, you will be refreshed and ready to go.

6. Delegate! It is not necessary to do everything yourself. In fact, it is not possible to do it alone. That is why there is a staff. Use them. Let them develop leadership skills.

7. Delegate, then let go. People who become administrators are often severe personal taskmasters. They expect things to be done well—maybe too well. It is crucial to realize that when tasks are delegated, things may be done differently than if you had done them yourself. Some may not be done as well. Some, however, may be done better. But if an administrator cannot let go, the task has not been truly delegated.

8. Decide what major issues you will tackle each year and stay focused on them. If other ideas come up, put them on a tickler list for next year. There will always be new things

to do, new ideas to promote. No one can do them all at one time, not even a principal.

9. Keep a list of ideas for future implementation.

10. Let go. Let go. Let go. The job is important, and it is necessary to do a good job. One has to keep it in perspective, however. The job is not the only thing that matters. No one wishes for more time at work when they are faced with the possibility of dying. Many people, however, wish they had spent more time with family or friends or doing things that gave them joy.

11. Seek activities outside of education. When at work, be at work. When away, be away. Maintain a balance and a perspective.

12. Schedule a positive part of the job into each day and each week. If classrooms observations are energizing, schedule them into the day. If walking the halls helps you stay connected with students, write that on the schedule. If you leave the enjoyable tasks to "when I have the time," more pressing concerns will eat into that time.

13. Do not apologize for setting priorities. Many people will want your attention. As the administrator, decide the focus of the building and your personal focus. Set priorities and explain to others that it is not possible for you to do everything.

14. Have fun!

Box 5.1   Journal

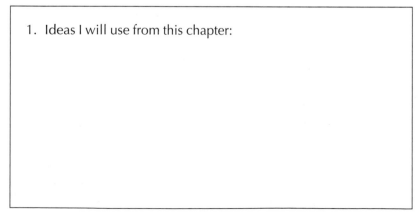

1. Ideas I will use from this chapter:

CHAPTER SIX

Developing Your Emotional Teflon

"No matter what you do, someone will not be happy" is a saying that should be hung in every administrator's office. Because an administrator makes decisions that affect many lives, it is impossible to make everyone happy. It is even difficult to make them mildly content. In fact, if everyone is happy, then the principal is not doing the job.

Those who are most unhappy are most likely to scream first, loudest, and longest. The opposite, however, is seldom true. People seldom run to the office to tell an administrator how happy they are. Certainly, there are those who go out of their way to be positive, to say thank you, and to talk about good things, but it seems to be true in a school that the bad news comes first and loudest. In a school, no news is indeed good news. An administrator learns quickly that there always key players who will give honest feedback, whether positive or negative. It is important to seek them out and get a read on the climate of the building.

EMOTIONAL TEFLON

Because so much of what an administrator hears is negative, it is difficult to stay upbeat. One needs to develop what I call *emotional Teflon*. One needs to be able to let negativity slide off. There are even times when it is helpful to imagine a Plexiglas shield between the head and heart so each can see what the other is doing but there is still protection.

People will come to an administrator with personal and professional problems. Therefore, much of the day is spent with negativity and problem solving. For example, a teacher comes before school to complain that no one rousts the morning smokers from the front of the building. (She did not say a word to them as she walked past because that's the job of an administrator.) Another teacher complains that the speakers are not working in his homeroom so he cannot hear announcements. Another complains that there are too many students in the halls instead of being in homeroom. This all takes place with the first "Good morning" of the day. Next a parent descends on the office to complain that she was never notified that her child had missed a class 10 times. The parent is angry with the teacher, the school, and, finally, the student, in the reverse order from what it should be. Few other occupations begin the day with such a negative jump-start.

Certain members of the staff will always have a negative comment, no matter what. Unfortunately, these teachers are the most vocal at staff meetings and in the staff lounge. In fact, there are teachers on staff that serve as a negative barometer. If they do not criticize something, it is always a pleasant shock. Those teachers who agree with administration and just do their job often sit quietly and tend to business. It is hard not to succumb to the overwhelming negativity.

The naysayers will have something to say about every policy, every meeting, and every decision. Such chronic complainers are not happy people. They believe that they are a voice for the rest of the staff and that they dare to say what others do not have the courage to say. That is not the case. Todd Whitaker (1999), author of *Dealing With Difficult Teachers*, believes these people are the

> *least* important people in your school. One of the faults in education and educational leadership is that we give too much power to these difficult people. . . . Too often we make decisions based on our least important people. (p. 19)

He also reminds administrators not to "argue with a difficult person. Realize that they have much more practice at it than you do" (p. 27).

It is sad to realize that such negativity feels more powerful than positive attitudes. It tends to feed on itself. Whitaker (1999) offers a simple guideline. "Always treat them [negative teachers] as though the entire staff were in the room. Realize that your positive and productive teachers want these negative staff members dealt with, but they want it done in a professional manner" (p. 27).

Build relationships with those on your staff who have balanced opinions. There are strong people who have a sense of propriety and go about their business. Yet, they will share concerns; sometimes it is necessary to go to them and ask, however, because they do not want to be seen as complainers. Work toward empowering this group. Build your plan around how it affects them. They are the true teacher leaders.

Administrative Burnout

Administrators who are described as "burnt out" are often accused of not listening to what teachers, students, and parents have to say. They are the ones who seem not to care, as though they were disconnected from issues and feelings. They seem to turn a deaf ear to issues because they have heard the same thing repeated time and again over the years.

When a person has been in a position for a number of years, there is repetition. Administrators as well as teachers hear the same laments over and over. The same issues keep recurring—class sizes are too large, kids are in the hall, the calendar is not respectful of teachers, and conference nights are inappropriately placed. It is indeed hard to stay fresh when the issues seem to be the same year after year.

For example, parents of incoming ninth graders who come to registration with their child for the first time are nervous, excited, and scared. They have a tendency to ask the same questions year after year. "How does homeroom work?" "How do students know how to find their classes?" "Do they have enough time between classes?" It is easy to lose sight of the fact that, although this is like Berenstain Bears' book, *Old Hat, New Hat*, the questions may be "old hat" for the principal but are "new hat" for parents.

Parents of new kindergarten students are much the same. They have the same questions because they have never been through this before and are anxious, excited, and nervous.

Because the patterns repeat, an administrator must be careful not to appear laissez-faire or uninvolved. One can use this repetition to be proactive instead. Principals could prepare a list of FAQs on parents' most frequently voiced concerns and send it with registration materials. Or an administrator could post an FAQ list about kindergarten on the school's Web site before the open house so that some of the questions have been answered and parents can relax.

If it feels tiresome and the excitement has gone from doing the task, then burnout has occurred. Find someone else to do the task or find a way to think about issues in a different way to put new life back into it and you. If an administrator can no longer see the issue from the other person's perspective, if the joy has gone, and the job feels claustrophobic, it may be time to do something else. There is no joy for anyone if people retire and still stay in the job.

DEVELOPING THE TEFLON—DILEMMA OR PROBLEM

How does one develop emotional Teflon so that issues do not become personal? One of the first steps is to decide if an issue is a problem or a dilemma. (This is discussed in Chapter 2.) Part of the process is to listen for the real message. Take the issue of students smoking in front of the building. If the administrator defines the issue as a problem, then he or she can assign more supervisors to be outside or can go personally. If the issue is really a dilemma because the teacher's purpose is to indirectly try to establish that the administrator is not seeing to his or her supervisory responsibility, then the issue is a dilemma with many more pieces. This issue can only be managed, not solved.

Besides defining issues as problems or dilemmas, there is also a need to decide what is under one's control and what is not. "Whose monkey is it?" is a line from an experienced administrator when he decides if the issue is something he should, or could, deal with. If someone came into his office to talk, vent, or co plain, that person was trying to get a "monkey off his or her back." Unfortunately, most people wanted that monkey to jump to his back so he would ask himself, "Whose monkey is it?" If the issue did not belong in the administrative office, he worked to realize that it was not his issue and that there was nothing for him to do. If the issue, however, did have elements that related to the building that needed to be dealt with, then he took it on. "Whose monkey is it?"

The hierarchical system of our schools has created a situation where some adults are sometimes treated almost like children.

"Dad" (or "Mom"), the administrator, is in charge, so it is the administrator's responsibility. However, sometimes we have to help our staff assume their own adult responsibility. When parents call and complain that a teacher has not contacted them, it is time to let the teacher know and to have the teacher contact the parents. It is not the job of the administrator to do the teacher's job. This is very difficult to do and takes developing Teflon, active listening, and self-awareness.

We know that teachers may never be entirely satisfied with what administrators do. Look at issues to see what the real issue is, assess it honestly, do what can be done, and then let it go. We have the mistaken belief that we, as teachers and as administrators, can fix and solve all issues as though they were problems, not dilemmas. It is important to stay invested, but it is also important to divest responsibility when appropriate. The hard part is to let go.

Suggestions

1. Know yourself. Care about people. Help people be the adults they are.

2. With difficult issues, sit down and think about them as though there is Plexiglas between the head and heart so that neither emotions nor the head alone is in charge, but that both work together.

3. Think about events from the perspective of, "What gift did I get from this experience?" "What will I do differently next time?" Using events as tools of the future helps an administrator stay engaged and fresh.

4. When patterns are repeated, such as open houses, curriculum nights, and so on, remember that this may be new for the participants, even though you have been through it a number of times. Think about it from their perspective. Treat it as though you were the participant and were experiencing it for the first time. What would you want to know? How would you want to be treated?

5. Practice listening for the real issue. When people start talking about an issue, they rarely begin with the bottom line. They usually start with the surface issue and only get to the real issue later, which usually takes about 20 minutes. When

people are presenting surface issues, their voices are airy, high, and from the throat. When the real issue comes out, the voice drops and becomes fuller because the air support is from the diaphragm. When the real issue comes out, people are afraid because they are more vulnerable. Treat this with sensitivity and care. There is more on this in Chapter 7.

6. Practice defining issues as problems or dilemmas. Problems beg for solutions, but dilemmas must be managed. We get tired and worn out by defining dilemmas as problems because we try to solve that for which there is no solution.

7. Exercise. Read. Play music. Walk. Do whatever it takes to keep the Teflon from getting scratched.

Box 6.1   Journal

1. When did I try to solve a dilemma?

2. What can I use from this chapter?

3. Are repeated events still fresh for me? Am I still excited about curriculum nights and parent conferences?

CHAPTER SEVEN

Maybe You Should Wear a Striped Shirt

Refereeing Conflict

Referees in many athletic contests wear black-and-white striped shirts so they are readily identified, as they declare "foul," "out," or "safe." Maybe an administrative uniform should include wearing a striped shirt because so much of what an administrator does is to mediate and referee conflict.

Of the hundreds of interactions throughout the day, most of them deal with some type of conflict.

- Pao wants more money from the gifted/talented budget but the coordinator does not believe that he needs it. You, as principal, get to mediate and explain to the coordinator why Pao needs that money.
- Marie and Avante, two guidance counselors, had an argument over who is responsible for the guidance office newsletter. The department chair calls you in as mediator to resolve the differences because the tiff is affecting the whole department.
- DaShawn had a verbal altercation with a teacher about a grade. The principal mediates between teacher and student.

- Ms. Hopkins is in your office demanding a 504 plan, a federally mandated program similar to an individual education plan, for her daughter, who has attention deficit hyperactivity disorder (ADHD). However, the child has not been officially diagnosed by a physician and cannot have services until that is done. Ms. Hopkins has consulted a private advocacy group that has told her to be forceful and demand that a school assessment take place. They did not make it clear to Ms. Hopkins, however, that the child needs a medical assessment before the school can implement any label, such as ADHD. Besides, a diagnosis of ADHD does not guarantee a 504. The principal gets to negotiate between the interests of the four parties—the student, the parent, school, and the advocacy group.
- The secretary is upset because Mr. Alvarez refused to answer his telephone in the early morning to avoid being asked to cover a class when there were not enough substitutes that day. The secretary wants the principal to talk to Mr. Alvarez.
- At the staff meeting, the administrator has the task of sharing news from the central office that the state has mandated training on recognizing mental illness in students. Staff members feel that this is a waste of time because teachers are not mental health professionals.

The list goes on and on. Conflict is a part of normal daily life. Teachers go into the profession because they want to teach. They like students and are excited about content areas. More important, they want to be liked and respected by students and coworkers alike. However, they do not want to deal with conflict. They believe that some of the most overt conflict, discipline, and angry parents are the domain of assistant principals and principals.

Teachers want conflict to be resolved in "the office," far away from their classrooms. In fact, most teachers fear an angry parent more than anything else because they were never trained to deal with anger or conflict. There is no university program that I know of that trains teachers and/or administrators to resolve disputes or defuse anger. Yet, any time there are two humans in the same spot at the same time, there is a possibility of conflict.

Administrators enter their jobs with the notion that they will be responsible for curricular issues, teacher evaluations, management of cleaning the school, supervision of school activities, dealing with parents, and dealing with discipline and attendance issues. However, the amount and degree of constant conflict, particularly its increase over the past 10 years, have been a great surprise. Several years ago, it was an occasional parent that presented a problem. In our current litigious society with the mentality that rules are for someone else but not for "my child," the conflict, particularly with parents, is a daily occurrence in many administrative positions.

Conflicts that arrive at an administrator's door are seldom simple because simple issues are usually solved before they get to the administrator. So the issues that arrive have gone through the layers of the bureaucracy unsuccessfully and/or have been passed on because no one wanted to deal with them.

Just as in negativity, the school's hierarchy is inverted when it comes to dealing with conflict. Administrators are at the bottom. Teachers, granted, have some conflict to manage, but the intensity and severity increase in geometric proportion at the administrative level. Administrators deal with so much conflict that by the time they go home, they do not want to hear the cats yowl at each other.

Such continual conflict takes its toll. What makes conflict even more difficult is that not every issue can be resolved to everyone's satisfaction. No one said that administration would be neat and orderly and would fit all the "in-basket" activities from courses in administration school. After all, we do not work in Garrison Keillor's Lake Woebegone schools.

What is also tiring are the "conflict junkies" who always look at a cup as half empty instead of half full. Some people create conflict, personally and professionally, no matter where they go. They get hooked on the endorphin high that comes from the rush of adrenaline that is produced during fights, fits of temper, and angry outbursts. They really do not want to resolve issues because they would not know how to welcome peace and joy into their lives. It may be necessary to put gentle but firm boundaries on such people because they will eat up a lot of time and energy.

In dealing with negative teachers, Todd Whitaker (1999) suggests that one strategy is to always "assume that difficult teachers want to do what is right . . . because it allows us to maintain relations with the challenging staff members at the same time that we are helping them grow by making them uncomfortable" (p. 51). What is key is stated well by Whitaker: "Relationships are everything to an effective principal" (p. 51).

LEVELS OF CONFLICT

Level 1 Conflict

Level 1 conflict contains those issues that can be dealt with relatively quickly. For example, the enrollment clerk has difficulty with Ms. Vujovich, who refused to turn in her grade sheets on time. Her lateness stops the entire process of scanning and printing grades. This conflict is easy to resolve because there is an obvious bottom line. An administrator tells Ms. Vujovich to turn in her grades on time because it is part of her professional responsibility, as outlined by her job description and the teacher code of ethics. If this happens again, the administrator needs to deal with it as insubordination in a formal write-up.

For Level 1 conflict, there is a right and wrong. Issues can be resolved by appealing to policy, laws, or commonly held values. For example, it is wrong for someone to hit another person. It is illegal to go through a red light. It is right that someone returns a stolen textbook. People, especially those who break society's rules, may disagree, but there are rules that we must abide by.

Level 2 Conflict

Level 2 conflict is more involved. There is a difference of opinion or values that are not clear-cut, and there is some responsibility on the part of each party. The perennial "he said, she said" type of argument would fit this category.

For example, two students have a fight over what one said about the other. There may be hurt feelings involved. The issue could have started months ago over a broken relationship. It could be that one of them is going out with the other one's former boyfriend or girlfriend. They may have called each other names. Or two students get into an argument on the playground over what happened at a birthday party. The conflict is not clear-cut, and the resolution involves admission of error—and possible hurt—by both parties.

This conflict takes time to resolve. Peer mediation strategies work. Strategies from Fisher, Ury, and Patton's (1991) *Getting to Yes* are beneficial. The following conflict resolution strategies are helpful:

1. First, there must be a mediator—often an administrator, social worker, or counselor—in the school who will listen to both sides. The mediator may listen to each side separately, or jointly so that each party can hear the other side.

2. Then the mediator needs to paraphrase to make certain that the real issue is out in the open. If each person agrees that the paraphrasing sums up the concern, the mediator can proceed. If not, then the mediator needs to ask further questions until clarity and honesty are reached.

3. When the issue is on the table, the mediator may need to probe even further to get at any underlying issues. What comes out first in a conflictual situation is usually just a surface issue. For Level 2 conflicts, the problem has built up over time and it will take time to probe for any underlying roots.

4. When the entire issue is out in the open, it is time to ask each person what it would take for the conflict to be over. Both parties need to state what they need. Then each party has to be able to fulfill that expectation. If they can, the conflict can be resolved. If not, the mediator will need to back up and reframe until each person is satisfied. If the issue is not correctly defined, one or more of the parties will not be able to give up the struggle.

5. A final closure activity is to get each person to agree that the conflict is over. For students, it is helpful at this point to give them pointers on what to say to their friends if friends try to stir it up again. It may be helpful to let them know what would happen if the conflict does crop up again so that the expectations are clear.

It often takes 45 to 60 minutes to mediate such occurrences and do it well. It takes ten to fifteen minutes to get the surface issues on the table. It may take another five to ten minutes to get at the real issue lying below the surface. Then each person needs a few minutes to state what he or she needs. Each person needs a few minutes to think and agree or disagree. It takes a few more minutes to restate what each person has agreed to and then leave the session. That is an hour or more of the day. When school is in session for only six to seven hours a day, it is easy to see how one conflict can eat away the time. It is not unusual to deal with several such conflicts during a week. Some schools train peers to perform this mediation. This relieves stress on adults and teaches students valuable skills, as well.

Level 2 conflicts took time to develop and take time to resolve because the conflicts are over issues that are value laden and, therefore, emotional. The process of coming to a solution that both people can live with cannot be rushed. If someone treats a Level 2 conflict as though it were Level 1, the conflict will resurface. For example, if two students are fighting and come to the office, simply telling them fighting is not allowed, suspending them, and sending them home will merely put the conflict on hold. There is a strong likelihood that the conflict will resurface either in the community or in school. It may even get worse, particularly if students drag their friends into it.

For adults, such conflicts may go underground. Students are more immediate and may have not learned to hide things as well as adults. If two teachers do not get along, instead of openly fighting as students may do, they tend to be more passive-aggressive— innuendos in the lounge or snide comments in meetings or in the hall.

Such conflict is detrimental to the morale of a staff. When administrators know about a longstanding conflict, it is better to bring the parties in to discuss it. Some administrators ignore such conflict, assuming that the teachers are adults and can deal with their own problems. Unfortunately, when paying attention to the culture of an organization it is important to deal with events that keep the culture from becoming healthy. Merely pushing it underground or ignoring it may cause the disharmony to fester and come out in other ways.

Disagreements are a healthy part of a human institution. Healthy relationships must have a chance to have conflict and then resolve it. Unhealthy conflict acts like a fungus and grows in dark places. It is the task of an administrator to bring such issues to light.

Level 3 Conflict

Level 3 conflict may not be able to be solved. It may be a dilemma, as opposed to a problem, as discussed in the previous chapter. Because dilemmas are rich in complexity, there may not be a permanent solution.

An example of a Level 3 conflict is when the district office allows too many students to enroll in the building. A school in the district might have space. However, the school is known for the quality of its programs, many parents have requested it, and the district wants to make parents happy. Unfortunately, the building is crowded. Teachers are complaining about the class size. Or, parents have exercised their rights for school choice. The classes are full, and the administrator wants to close the school to new enrollments, but the district office is not supportive.

The district wants to allow parents their choice of schools to help meet the wishes of the community. However, the staff of the school want to deliver the quality program without being overwhelmed. Their perception is that a crowded school is not educationally sound. Both groups have sound arguments.

This conflict is a dilemma that can only be managed, not solved. The administrator in charge will have to make some decisions about lunches, classroom assignments, and itinerant teachers. Some teachers will not have their own classroom. Some teachers will have to share. Teachers will have to order more books.

There will be issues throughout the school year because of more discipline referrals, the inability to get all students into computer labs at one time, and so on. The building administrator becomes a manager of details instead of an instructional leader.

Level 3 conflict is a dilemma that must be managed by a variety of methods. It is frustrating, however, because the conflict appears in so many different arenas. Lower level conflicts can be solved. However, most of what happens in schools are Level 2 or Level 3 conflicts, which are more time-consuming and stressful.

Hawthorne Effect

The Hawthorne effect is the belief that some issues may improve simply because of the attention paid to them. For example, there are signs posted on some city streets that say "accident-free zone." Studies show that there were fewer accidents in those areas, but not because of more police intervention or lower speed limits. The only thing that changed was the sign. The Hawthorne effect was working.

Sometimes, school issues work themselves out because someone paid attention. Attendance is a good example. There is no easy answer to the problem of getting students to school on time. Teachers will feel validated, however, if an attendance committee is formed, policies are changed, or new ideas are developed because that acknowledges their daily struggle to get students to class so they can learn. But we know that attendance policies are dilemmas. There is no one solution to the issue, but the Hawthorne effect helped to create culture where the teachers felt the administration was paying attention to issues that are important to them.

The staff perceive that the administrators will devote energy to initiatives the administrators deem important. If an administrator wants to resolve a conflict between members of a department, then it is perceived that the resolution of that conflict is an important issue. If an administrator ignores such a conflict, it will be perceived that the administrator does not give it a high priority.

It is important to choose issues wisely. Merely paying attention may help get a problem resolved. But it may not. Conflict is normal. When people are comfortable, they become complacent and have no reason to do anything differently. It is only when someone becomes uncomfortable that there is motivation to change. Therefore, conflict can be seen as a powerful change agent. Instead of fighting it, we can embrace it as a means to a new beginning—it could be an outlier to change.

HEALTHY CONFLICT

Not all conflict is bad. Conflict may serve a healthy purpose by allowing issues to be presented and resolved. A certain amount of turmoil can be an outlier or strange attractor to new understanding and healing, but only if people are willing to deal directly with the conflict.

Suggestions

1. Learn how to resolve conflict, if not familiar with doing so. Excellent resources are *Getting Past No: Negotiating With Difficult People* by Ury (1991) and *Getting to Yes: Negotiating Agreement Without Giving In* by Fisher et al. (1991).

2. Learn to define issues as dilemmas or problems. The method of framing the issue will determine the type and amount of initiatives available for its solution.

3. When dealing with angry or upset people, realize that the first important step is to listen. What they really want is someone to hear their viewpoint.

4. To deal with conflict "junkies," schedule them at a time when there is a limited amount of time to listen. Put firm boundaries on them and yet acknowledge their concerns. It could be damaging in the teacher network if they perceive they are being brushed off, but it is not necessary to give them all the time they *think* they need. Schedule them for the last half hour before they have to be back in their classroom, for example, so that there is a built in time limit.

5. Recognize that conflict gives us lessons to learn. Each problem solved and each conflict resolved moves us along on the journey to a mature understanding of and the ability to work with people.

6. Conflict is healthy. It is a positive interchange when differing opinions lead to a new understanding. Conflict is good!

Box 7.1   Journal

1. Describe a personal conflict that became a good learning experience.

2. When was the last time I thought of conflict as "good"?

3. How will defining conflicts as Level 1, 2, or 3 help me in dealing with issues?

CHAPTER EIGHT

Everything You Didn't Know About Adult Learners

In college, we learned about stages of child development, but we never studied adult development. However, we do not stop developing and learning once we reach age 20 or even 40. Because administrators work with adults, it is important to think of them as learners also.

The idea of stages of adult psychosocial development was popularized and brought to the forefront by such writers as Gail Sheehy, author of *Passages* (1974/1997), and Dan Levinson, author of *The Seasons of a Man's Life* (1978). Sheehy observed that men and women experience the same stages of adult development, albeit asynchronously. She believed that there appear to be more "outer restrictions and inner contradictions for women during the first half of life" (p. 19). The opposite appears to be true for men. This was important because Sheehy believed that the "prizes of our society," such as promotions, tend to be for outer, not inner, achievement.

Levinson's (1978) work, done with 40 adult men, describes four stages of development:

- Stage 1—childhood and adolescence from ages 3 to 17
- Stage 2—early adulthood from ages 22 to 40

- Stage 3—middle adulthood, from ages 45 to 60
- Stage 4—late adulthood, beyond the age of 65

He described a phenomenon he called "transition," which function as times to reflect on the previous stage and to prepare for the next one. The transitions, particularly important times, last from four to five years.

It is important to understand the stages of adult development because teachers and staff within our buildings may be experiencing any of the stages, from Stages 2 through 4. In Stage 2, adults are in the "greatest contradiction and stress" (Levinson, 1978, p. 22). Adults are struggling to find their place in society and personally. This is the time of coupling, raising families, investing in homes, and getting further education. It is a time of great accomplishments and great frustration.

Stage 3, middle adulthood, brings a change. This is the time that some people have called a "midlife crisis," when they begin to realize that there is a shift in life. Human bodies began to wear down. Professionally, many people have reached a peak of satisfaction. Families may be growing up and leaving home. It is the time when people begin to look toward retirement and the calming of life, instead of looking toward challenges and excitement.

Stage 4 brings people to retirement, to leaving a profession that has defined their identity, and to facing physical ailments. It is exciting to some and dreadful to others.

As administrators, we expect to deal with children and adolescents who are in Stage 1. We are ill prepared to deal with most of the adults on our staff and our parents, who are in the other three stages.

Sheehy (1974/1997) and Levinson (1978) brought attention to looking at adult behavior from a viewpoint of what Strauss and Howe (1991) called "cohort-group biography," meaning that we "understand ourselves as groups of like-aged friends with a distinctive collective story" (p. 45). The research on cohorts is "still a young science" (Strauss & Howe, 1991, p. 49). What the work of such people as Sheehy, Levinson, and Strauss and Howe has done is to help us think differently about dealing with adults, that they are not all the same once they reach maturity, and that adults do learn differently from children.

ADULT LEARNERS

Administrators deal with adults constantly as we provide professional development, curriculum nights, and parent information sessions. Stephen Lieb (n.d.), from South Mountain College, described the work of Malcolm Knowles, who used the work of Piaget and Erikson to study the adult learner. Knowles recognized that adults learn best with what he called "self-directed inquiry," which is the foundation for using the constructivism of the 1990s.

Some other characteristics of adult learners are as follows:

- Adult learners are autonomous and self-directed. They will want to learn what they see as useful, either personally or professionally.
- Adults want to know what they are going to get out of any situation. What is the goal? How is any new program going to affect their daily lives? Is it going to mean more work? More paperwork?
- Adults want to learn things that will affect them directly.
- Adults do not want to waste time. Time is seen as teachers' most valuable commodity because they never have enough time to get the entire curriculum covered, grade papers, or contact parents.
- Adults want to be treated with respect by using their time well and providing breaks.

Practical Strategies for Honoring Adult Learners

1. Send out agendas prior to meetings and stick to them. Start and end the meetings on time—ending a little early is even better.

2. Be well prepared for any meeting. Have background materials ready to hand out. If this information is helpful for a good discussion, send the information out prior to the meeting so people can read it before the meeting.

3. Teachers have less tolerance for boredom than do students. When doing staff development, remember to structure the time in a manner that recognizes how people learn. For example, in an hourlong session, the first 20 minutes are the most important. The next most important time is the last 10 minutes, which

should be spent summarizing and concluding the purpose of the meeting. The middle 30 minutes are the low point of learning. Just as in a classroom, it is important to structure this time as activity, movement, dialogue, or interaction.

4. Adults need a physical break every hour so they can get up and move around. Teachers are less tolerant than their students for inactivity because their profession requires them to be moving. So do not expect them to sit any longer than 45 to 50 minutes without a break.

5. It is difficult to get adults to refocus after a break. Plan an activity that gets them engaged.

6. Balance instruction with activity. We know the value of cooperative group work. However, there are times when adults want to learn. They are comfortable with listening and learning if the presenter knows what he or she is talking about. They will not, however, be willing to listen to people who does not know what they are talking about.

7. Make group work purposeful. Do not just put people in groups because someone said cooperative learning is effective. Structure the group work so that there is a task and a meaningful outcome expected. Do not have groups where the instruction is "Discuss this at your table." This feels like the presenter is trying to kill time to earn a consulting fee. The task should be something that has a required outcome and will help move the discussion forward, not just recap what was presented earlier. Adults do not want to share their ignorance; they want to make meaningful use of their time.

8. Structure staff meetings in a manner that is reflective of professional development opportunities. Have information prepared, watch the time, change activities, and make the activities meaningful.

9. Provide a wide variety of learning opportunities for teachers. Support their individual interests. Be supportive by finding money and time when they need them for their professional growth. Then get out of their way and let them do what they do best—teach.

GENERATIONAL CONSIDERATIONS

In addition to knowing about adult learners, it is important to understand the characteristics of the different generations in our workplace. Because we did not consider the adult stages of learning in the past—because once someone was adult, that person was lumped with all other adults—we also did not think about the different forces that shaped different generations and how this affects their daily work behavior.

Zemke, Raines, and Filipczak (2000), authors of *Generations at Work: Managing the Clash of Veterans, Boomers, Xers, and Nexters in Your Workplace,* felt that the topic of generations was important because "at no previous time in our history have so many and such different generations with such diversity been asked to work together shoulder to shoulder, side by side, cubicle to cubicle" (p. 10).

The discussion of this topic is not meant to be ageist but is merely trying to offer administrators understanding as they work with different groups. Understand that this is a quick overview. Entire books are written on the topic, if someone wants to read further. It is important to be aware of some of the differences because those differences are reflected in how we design professional development, how we hear what people are saying, and how we understand the needs of people.

Veterans

Members of the veteran generation, born between 1922 and 1943, are nearing the end of their work experience, although they continue to work after retirement and still exert influence. They are

- Conformers
- Consistent
- Disciplined
- Past oriented
- Believers in law and order
- Fiscally conservative
- Invested in hierarchies and chains of command
- Loyal
- Not as technologically savvy or interested as some other generations (Zemke et al., 2000, pp. 36–49)

Baby Boomers

The baby boomers, born between 1943 and 1960, are redefining our culture as they move through it. Some of their characteristics are as follows:

- Optimistic
- Willing to break society's rules throughout their lives by protesting, by using personal chemicals such as marijuana and LSD, and now by resisting the aging process
- Workaholic—60 hours a week, no problem
- Team players
- Interested in self-actualization reading, activities, and explorations
- Working longer than other generations
- Lifelong learners (Zemke et al., 2000, pp. 63–92)

Generation Xers

The next group, Generation Xers (although they resist the label) were born between 1960 and 1980, were raised in the shadow of the boomers. Although somewhat difficult to describe, some of their indicators are as follows:

- Resistant of labels and categories, including the title of Gen X
- Self-reliant
- Trying for balance—life is not all about work
- Seeking a sense of family—reacting to the fact their parents spent a lot of time at work and see the problem with that
- Informal—do not have to wear suits and ties to demonstrate power and knowledge
- Nontraditional in orientation about time and space—they get the job done, regardless of the 40-hour workweek. They should not have to come in by 8 a.m. or leave by 4 p.m.; as long as the work gets done, who cares?
- Casual in their approach to authority
- Skeptical
- Technologically very savvy
- Willing to change careers, not just jobs
- Self-starting in unique businesses (e.g., Bill Gates)

- More egalitarian than hierarchical
- Not as team oriented as boomers and vets because they are so independent
- Changing rules of communication with their use of technology (Zemke et. al., 2000, pp. 98–102)

Nexters

The next generation, called the Nexters or Generation Y, was born between 1980 and 2000. Some characteristics are as follows:

- Reflective of the values of the veterans as they are more conservative and believe in a stricter moral code, with a resurgence of belief in manners
- Optimistic about the future and realistic about the present
- Resilient and productive, hardworking
- Demanding in the workplace—demanding pay equity, for example
- Relatively new to the workplace, so it is too early to know how they will influence it (Zemke et al., 2000, pp. 126–149)

IMPLICATIONS

Remember that the following comments are generalizations. They are meant to be thought provoking, not proscriptive. In some places, veteran employees are still in the workplace, particularly in superintendencies. Although their influence is fading, their style of leadership and value system are still felt because some are recycling into superintendencies as interims, even after they have formally retired.

Much of the leadership that is facing retirement is from the boomer generation. The aspiring administrators are Gen Xers. There is a definite difference in style. Plus, the veterans and boomers have gone through most of their careers without the current climate of accountability and technology. Many current superintendents still rely on voice mail and secretaries and are not as comfortable with PDAs e-mails, and data drill-down software. Some may use this technology, but it is not as easy or familiar as it is to the next generation.

Another difference among the groups is the attitude toward the workday and workweek. Boomers entered the profession when salaries were low and when teachers took on extra responsibilities, such as sponsoring a club, without any extra pay. They did, and still do, take pride in working long hours (Zemke et al., 2000, p. 77). The Gen Xers strive for more of a balance and are willing to put limits around the amount of hours they will work. This has caused some friction in hiring younger administrators who do not feel that they should have to work a 60- to 70-hour week to cover all the activities. Can't someone else be hired to do that?

Because veterans and boomers were raised in times that dealt with genocide, prejudice, the civil rights era, and the Vietnam War, they still carry the feeling of human rights in their attitudes toward students and staff.

However, the Gen Xers were affected by an unstable economy, high inflation, and uncertain job futures. They were raised during the Nixon era and the Reagan era, and they "aren't so much against authority as simply unimpressed by it" (Zemke et al., 2000, p. 101). They believe that just because something is past practice is no reason to continue doing it if it does not serve a purpose. They are more comfortable in changing rules and shaping new traditions, which causes anxiety to those who find comfort in doing what has been done in the past.

Loyalty and attitude toward extra work is one way that differences appear. Veterans are fiercely loyal and will work for the same organization for their entire career. Boomers entered the workforce when getting a job in education was a good thing. As teachers, they were expected to do a lot without being reimbursed, such as coaching some activities, chaperoning, and advising clubs. Gen Xers have a different attitude. They want to be paid for after-hour duties; otherwise, they often decline. They would rather use their free time in a manner they choose, such as with family, than work for nothing.

Gen Xers enjoy their free time and have many interests. Boomers have worked many hours and find much of their identity in their job. Retirement for boomers is sometimes difficult because they have not taken time to develop pastimes outside of work, so they get another job.

Technology and multitasking are other differences. Boomers were themselves told and often told their children to turn off the

TV while they were studying because they could not do two things at once. Gen Xers prove that wrong constantly. They can instant message or e-mail, listen to music, and talk to someone at the same time.

The use of technology has created a demand on schools for more information and for it to be almost instantaneous. Parents want to see their child's daily attendance and grades online each night. They want to monitor what their child eats each week by looking at that online. There is an unwritten expectation that voice mails are answered within 24 to 48 hours or sooner because cell phones are accessible at all times, e-mails within a day, and letters within two days. Not all groups are equally comfortable with these demands.

SUMMARY

It is important for administrators to understand the life stages of the adults in the system. It is important to understand how adults learn and to pay attention to that as staff meetings are designed, professional development is planned, and committees are structured.

It is important to realize that we are not all the same as adults. We have had different events that happened in our culture that shaped our cohort. Traumatic events such as the Kennedy assassinations, the *Challenger* explosion, and the destruction of the Twin Towers are events that shape each of us, depending on our age at the time of the occurrence and how it affected our life's path. It is important to use all this information to help understand the best way to work with and support our people.

Box 8.1   Journal

1. What evidences do I see of different generations in my workplace?

2. How can I be more responsive to adult learners?

3. Other ideas from this chapter. . . .

CHAPTER NINE

Looking Into the Mirror of Humor

Just think of the material for stand-up comedians if they walked around schools for a week. Just visualize prom, when the girls are wearing their strapless dresses and are dancing up a storm. Each time they leave the dance floor, they hike up the dress. Think of a parody of middle school kids walking down the hall in their platform shoes, trying to act so grown-up but struggling to walk without falling flat on their faces. Think of our little kids learning to walk in line for the first time.

Just imagine a staff meeting when the photography teacher is getting photo mats ready for a show. He brought his materials with him so that he could work during the meeting. Another teacher is complaining about the kids in the hall, and each time he starts to talk, the photography teacher just happens to yank on a roll of duct tape and it "quacks" in rhythm to the complaining teacher. After a while, the staff catch on and start to snicker, and the photography teacher looks up, is a little embarrassed, and then gives the tape one big yank, one big "quack," and everyone laughs.

If we looked at the daily life of a school through the eyes of an outsider, think of the stories we could write. What if we were not so serious and were able to use humor to be reflective, like a mirror, to help us keep perspective? When was the last time you really laughed so hard that your sides hurt? Can you even remember? Kids do that all the time, adults not as often.

Laughter is a release, much like exercise or meditation. Laughter acts like an internal "massage" to release endorphins that, in turn, reduce stress. One of the first people to discover the healing properties of laughter was Norman Cousins (1979), in *Anatomy of an Illness.* Since then, many studies have documented its healing properties.

Loretta LaRoche (1998), author of *Relax, You May Only Have a Few Minutes Left,* said that laughter affects the body emotionally and physically. Laughter boosts the immune system. LaRoche found that people with a sense of humor do better in their jobs and tend to be more creative, less rigid, and more willing to consider and embrace new ideas and methods.

Elementary teachers, as a whole, like to have fun and play with their students. Middle school and junior high teachers have to be zany to stay sane. They have a tendency to dress in gross costumes at Halloween or are willing to tell stories in science that gross out people. High school teachers tend to be the most serious lot of the three levels. They need to learn to be more playful.

Paul G. Young (2004), author of *You Have to Go to School— You're the Principal,* believes that

> people also benefit from laughter. They don't like working for people who frown and always appear too serious. Principals who can create a school culture where laughing is appreciated and accepted will realize higher performance, from adults and students both. . . . People will enjoy being there. (p. 156)

The unconscious physical power of smiling can be demonstrated to a class or a staff. Have a volunteer stand up and hold out his or her arms. Tell that person to resist with all his or her might as another person tries to push the arms down. Then draw a big frowning face on the whiteboard and have the volunteer stare at it for 30 seconds. Then have that person hold out his or her arms again and resist as the second person pushes them down. The arms invariably collapse, much to the volunteer's surprise who thought he or she was resisting hard.

Next draw a happy face on the whiteboard. Have the volunteer stare at it for 30 seconds and then hold out the arms again. Have the other person push down on the arms. The arms will stay up. The volunteer will be able to describe the difference his or her body felt during the experience. It will work whatever order you use, whether sad first, then happy, or in reverse order.

An observer will be able to watch the volunteer and see the difference in body language. Watching the frowning face, the shoulders slump, the face sags, and the brow knits. Watching the happy face, the face smoothes out and hands relax.

Research shows that stress decreases the ability to learn because the limbic system of the brain is on alert and cuts off the ability to gain and retain information. There is power in positive thinking. Positive people seek out other positive people. Students request teachers who make them feel good—those with the happy faces.

A school community, like a family, needs positive times together to play and laugh. Administrators can create some of those opportunities for a sense of camaraderie and joy.

If life were a song, it should be reggae or calypso, not a dirge.

SUGGESTIONS

1. Laugh. If you smile, people smile in return.

2. Go see funny movies.

3. Bring fresh flowers to work. The smell and sight of them makes people smile and wonder about a special occasion. If it is just a regular day, people feel good anyway.

4. Learn to see the paradoxes of life. The more one works, the more one needs to play. The more one cries, the more one needs to laugh.

5. Find things that make you smile and laugh. Humor is so individualized that it is difficult to suggest one thing to please everyone. But find what gives you joy and seek it out, whether it's playing with your children or grandchildren, watching sitcoms, or watching old slapstick movies.

Box 9.1   Journal

1. What makes me laugh?

2. When was the last time I laughed so hard my stomach hurt?

CHAPTER TEN

Power Is Like Love: The More You Give Away, the More You Have

P ower and love are paradoxes. People have opinions as to what they are, but it is difficult to have a clear-cut definition. In this time of collaboration and site teams, it is important to talk about the different types of power because they are often diffuse. Therefore, it is important to talk about these overriding, nebulous topics because their interaction can make one successful—or not.

TYPES OF POWER

In the hierarchy of schools, the power of position within a building rests with the principal. Each principal has a different interpretation of how to use this power. French and Raven (1959, pp. 155–164) defined five types of social power:

1. Reward power is that which promises rewards if someone performs. Teachers earn more money if they get more credits.

2. Coercive power is that which forces someone to act against his or her will. Teachers have to cover study hall even if they do not want to because it is a contractual agreement.

102

3. Legitimate power is that which is assigned a certain position. The principal can direct teachers. Positional power such as this is not as important to Gen Xers. They are more willing to work with someone who demonstrates expert power.

4. Referent power is that which comes from a constituent's belief in the power of the superior. Hitler used his referent power to keep his SS guards from revolting.

5. Expert power is that which comes from proficiency. If someone is the expert on authentic assessment in the building, that person has power.

The historical authoritarian-father image of the principal relied heavily on reward, coercive, and legitimate power. Principals could coerce staff and students to perform because cultural mores allowed it. Subordinates were expected to follow orders, and they did so with little challenge. However, this model is gradually changing.

True leaders are able to motivate by the willingness of people to follow. Hence, a paradox. Leaders can lead only if others follow. To use an extreme example, cult leaders such as Hitler or James Jones would have had no power if people had not given it to them. If they had been ostracized as nutty radicals, they would have been marginalized and ineffective.

The type of collaborative and instructional leadership that works in today's schools relies on referent and expert power, particularly on expert power. Certainly, there is still reward power in operation. The teachers who take on challenging roles are less likely to be asked to perform hall duty. Or if a teacher is the adviser on the yearbook, she or he may be given a last hour prep. Those are definite rewards.

Referent power is exercised when teachers work with the principal because the principal is the boss. But referent power is often emotional. There are inspiring leaders whom people will follow no matter what. To be effective, a principal needs some of the awe surrounding referent power because teachers are more likely to work hard with a principal they see as having a personal strength, expertise, or charisma. Teachers are more likely to be passive-aggressive with a principal they see as ineffective, even if the person is still the boss.

The principal also needs expert power through understanding systems, best practice, pedagogy, discipline, curriculum, staff personalities, and the interaction of all of the above. Teachers expect a principal to understand the daily occurrences in a classroom. They also expect the principal to be intelligent, well read, well spoken, a good administrator, and creative.

Teachers want principals to use their expert power to perform the administrative tasks that facilitate a well-run building so that teachers can teach without being bogged down with time-consuming administrative tasks. Because most teachers love teaching and dislike politics, policies, and administrative tasks, it is difficult to get them involved in some tasks on site councils that they perceive as administrative in nature. Teachers will say, "If I wanted to be an administrator, I'd be one. I don't want to do that. I want to teach!"

Respect or Power

So much of what we mistake for power is actually respect. For example, a teacher gives students a ten-minute reading assignment. Most students are done in five minutes. However, they sit for the next five minutes because they respect the teacher. This teacher has referent power. In a classroom directly across the hall with a different teacher who is not respected, those same students would be talking or doing other homework.

True power comes from respect. Unfortunately, many people equate power with control and force. As administrators, we get more done by being respected for our expertise and skill than by using force.

Personal Power

Some people work hard to have power. They want a job at the top of the management flowchart so that they will be in charge. They think that a title or position will bring them respect. However, that type of power is illusory because most authentic or real power is personal. Power attached to a position or title has severe limitations. If the title is gone, does the person lose all power?

Personal power comes from a level of expertise, knowledge, personal strength, caring, and understanding, which create a synergy labeled as power. Personal power is something that does not disappear with a new job title.

Someone who has personal power is also able to empower others, like the Level 5 leader of Collins (2001) in *Good to Great*.

The more power one gives away, the more one has. If there is a task to do, and the leader assigns it to two others who complete the task, then power is shared and others are empowered, as long as the leader gives credit for the work to those who completed it.

The idea of trying to grasp or hold on to power is an idea based in fear—fear of losing self-control, self-image, or self-worth. If buildings are administered in that fashion of grasping, then no one works as a team to share and build a sense of unity. If buildings are guided by sharing and empowering, then all are elevated to a leadership and ownership role.

Power Struggles

Power struggles are unnecessary. During a power struggle, the opposing parties want to punish. If the struggle is between teacher and student, the teacher wants to know what type of punishment the student will receive.

Punishment is usually an external rule or consequence applied by someone older, stronger, and bigger. Punishment such as that is usually fear or shame based. It may work temporarily, as long as the punisher remains older, bigger, and stronger. If there is no relationship, people resort to force, such as punishment. However, what really changes behavior is if there are consequences that affect the relationship between the parties—it is the respect that I have for you that gives you power over me.

Power struggles surface when there is a lack of respect between the parties and a contest about how much one party can force the other party to conform. Power struggles surface when someone feels scared or threatened. Parties enter a contest with the mistaken perception that "winning" is important. But winning also implies that someone has to lose, which is precisely what happens in a power struggle. For example, a teacher told several students to be quiet in the hallway outside of his door. They did not. He went out and yelled at them. They yelled back. He sent them to the office. They did not go. He called for help, and a security guard was sent. The students then went to the office.

He never asked them to be quiet. He never related to them as responsible students. Instead, he ordered them to cooperate. When they did not, he "upped the ante." The students knew that their behavior was inappropriate. They did not have respect for the teacher, so they did not give him power over them. Instead, both parties escalated the problem, trying to win. The teacher, as an adult, should have been smarter and not set up the struggle. He literally could not force them to be quiet or to move to the administration. Because the students happened to respect the security guard, they allowed him to take them to the office. They could have run, fought, yelled, screamed, or been otherwise obnoxious, but they were not.

The teacher could have gone to the students and asked them to be quiet. He could have told the students that their noise was so loud that his students could not hear the morning announcements. He could have asked for their help instead of ordering them to be quiet. He could have used strategies that were based on relationships and caring, rather than on force and positional power. Instead, he pushed, and they pushed back. He pushed again; they pushed back harder.

What would have worked better in this situation was for someone to sidestep the issue. Force begets force. If, however, the other person had moved aside when the first person pushed, there would have been nothing for the first person to push against. The struggle would be defused. Asking for help is one way to defuse. Using humor is another. Not responding to taunts is another. Reframing the problem and listening for the real issue is another. Adults need to examine the real issue and sidestep deliberate attempts at push and shove.

Power struggles never work because they are based on coercion and fear. There is no need to create such situations to try to have power over another because we have all the power we need. No one can take that away from us.

Suggestions for How to Disseminate Power

1. Give staff, students, and parents credit publicly and privately for what they do. The power of a staff is also the power of the administrator. The more one gives away, the more one has.

2. Sidestep power struggles. Look for the real issue and deal with it. Do not get involved when someone is having a bad day and taking it out on everyone around.

3. Power is more of a belief than a practice, just like love. Remember the paradox: Give it away to get it back.

Box 10.1   Journal

1. Reflections on this chapter:

2. What is the source of my "power"?

CHAPTER ELEVEN

Leading in the Age of Accountability

W e are in an age of accountability and standards. We are measured and compared with schools within a district, state, and nation. The push has been heightened by the latest update of the Elementary and Secondary Education Act (ESEA) of 1965, which is now known as the No Child Left Behind (NCLB) Act of 2001. Gerald Bracey, professor, researcher, and author, has said that a better acronym is No Child Left Untested or LNSS (Let No School Succeed) (Bracey, 2003, p. 5).

As a gross generalization, each state is to develop standards and tests aligned with those standards to measure annual progress made by *all* students. The state is then to publish the information in an understandable format so the public can make informed decisions about their children's education. However one feels about the law, it is important to understand the key facts of accountability and how to live with it in a manner that helps administrators keep their sanity and integrity.

ASSETS OF THE NCLB

For whatever reason, not to be debated here, the federal government is more actively intrusive than in the past. The federal government enacted the Elementary and Secondary Education

Act in 1965, which is revisited every five to seven years. The law defines federal involvement in public education, a role that has become increasingly proscriptive.

When the most recent version of the ESEA, commonly called the No Child Left Behind Act, was signed into law in 2001, the federal government instituted more consequences for public schools than ever before. There are proficiency targets that must be met each year, as measured by state tests, so that all students are proficient in reading, math, and science by the year 2014. For in-depth information about the law and its many ramifications, go to www.ed.gov, a wonderful resource. In all likelihood, various aspects and interpretations of the law will change over time, so it is important to stay current.

Several key components of the legislation are important and will probably be retained in some form. All schools must make adequate yearly progress (AYP) toward the goal of proficiency. Teachers must be highly qualified. Paraprofessionals must be highly qualified. Parents have the right to some options if their child attends a school that has not made AYP for two years. Each state must develop standards and tests that measure progress toward those standards. Each state must develop report cards about schools for parents. How each of these is accomplished may be fine-tuned over time, but most people feel that these large ideas will remain.

What was different about NCLB, in comparison to other enactments of ESEA, were the escalating consequences for public schools if they continue to lag behind in their goals.

The assets and faults of the legislation are debated daily in journals, newspapers, and in the teachers' lounges. There are some good points to the legislation:

1. Education is being discussed routinely.

2. There are conscious efforts to look at data to make certain all students are making progress.

3. Schools are being forced to look at data in a manner they have not done before.

4. There is an emphasis on teacher quality and a recognition that a highly qualified teacher makes a difference.

However. . . .

1. Once again education is being politicized and debated by everyone. Everyone is an expert because they have been through school. However, because one has been to a doctor does not make one skilled enough to be a doctor. The criticisms that are being levied against educators one more time are coming from politicians, not educators, who use education as a platform to sway public opinion, not necessarily improve education. They rush to become called "education governors" or "education presidents." They use education as an emotional, political platform instead of as a forum to change public policy for public good.

There are conscious efforts to look at various student populations and to disaggregate data to make certain all students are making progress. First, we have the myth that public education in the United States is the great equalizer of our melting pot. We have bought into the idea that if all students are educated, all of them have the same opportunity to be successful.

2. That is a fallacy. Schools cannot entirely erase the effects of generational poverty, the lack of education because someone has lived in a refugee camp for four years, or the effects of being Black in a racist society, for example. Schools can ameliorate the effects of some of those things but cannot be responsible for curing the ills of society. Addressing poverty, homelessness, joblessness or underpaying jobs, medical needs, and so on are larger issues that must be addressed on all levels—national, state, and local.

Students are in school only six hours a day from at least the ages of six to 16. But they spend a lot more time in front of a television than they do in a classroom.

3. Schools are looking at data in a manner they have never done before. Before technology, we did not have the tools to use to look at data in a timely fashion. We still do not have training for teachers and administrators as to how to interpret all these data.

One of the sources of data is annual testing. Using annual, one-snapshot tests is hardly an indication of growth. The tests compare this year's third graders with next year's third graders. That is like comparing cows to giraffes.

When schools use value-added tests, such as those designed by the Northwest Evaluation Association (NWEA), teachers are able to look at individual students and monitor student progress.

The teacher is able to adjust instruction accordingly in a meaningful fashion. When we can look at growth for a particular student, then we can use those data to change instruction for that student, use differentiation strategies, and honor learning styles. Tests that lump all third graders together to be assessed against next year's third graders do not help us change instruction.

However, the national "wonks" believe standardized tests are meaningful because students can be compared equally across states. The current system, however, allows each state, under the guise of local control, to design its own standards and tests. Therefore, it is not possible to compare Arkansas with California. So the federal government decided that all schools who receive Title I funding must be tested by the National Association of Educational Progress (NAEP) so there are interstate comparisons. Another test. . . .

However, the NAEP, according to the Center for Research on Evaluation, Student Standards, and Testing (CRESST); the General Accounting Office; and the National Academy of Science—as well as to individual psychometricians such as Lyle Jones of the University of North Carolina—agree that the "methods used [by the NAEP] are flawed, confusing, internally inconsistent, and lack evidence of validity. Most important, the results don't accord with any other data" (Bracey, 2003, p. 3).

4. There is recognition that teacher quality matters. However, the current teacher shortage, particularly in some subject matters and some geographic areas, allow states to establish their own criteria for "highly qualified." Even the law allows people to have an alternative entry into the teaching profession by being mentored by a teacher or having a certain level of experience.

What we find over and over is that there is no replacement for someone trained in content and pedagogy. It is not enough to know "stuff," a person must know how to teach. And, no, not everyone can.

5. If truly no child should be left behind or, as some say, no child's behind is left (Bracey, 2003, p. 5), then all schools should be held to the same standards—public schools, nonpublic schools, charter schools, and home schools. Currently, only public and charter schools get their results published on a statewide report card every year. How do parents of nonpublic schools know if their children are making a year's worth of growth? By grades? By

growing a year older? How do home schoolers know if they are achieving?

All home school students who reenter our system come with straight As. Are only the brightest students being educated at home? Or is one-on-one attention the way that all students can learn at that level? If that is true, we need a lot more money for education to close the achievement gap. If we could have one-on-one instruction for some of our poorest students, our refugee students, what progress we could make. That would be fun!

6. Holding schools hostage, not accountable, on the basis of one test per year is nonsensical. Business and industry do not hold themselves accountable based on quality control conducted once a year. Car manufacturers do not test drive one car once a year. So why do we try to be mechanistic with human beings?

Most educators have no problem with being held accountable because educators want students to learn. However, they do want a level playing field and want *all* schools held to the same standards. Currently, in our society, those who are rich enough to send a child to a private school or who can stay home to educate the children are not accountable. Are they left behind?

What Can an Administrator Do?

It is important to look at the school as a system of interlocking parts. There are several key items that we know increase student achievement. Dr. Donald Fielder (2003), in his book *Achievement Now! How to Assure No Child Is Left Behind,* suggests the following:

- Increase time on task
- Have a rigorous pre-K–12 aligned curriculum
- Use data to target areas of need
- Use highly qualified teachers in a professional manner—give them time to look at student data, provide meaningful professional development, and relieve them of meaningless pressure so they can teach
- Involve parents
- Lower class size (pp. 13–181)
- Provide meaningful leadership and vision by providing a strong focus on academic achievement

The greatest task for the administrator is the last one—to provide leadership and focus for teachers to do their job. To do so, the administrator must focus on systems thinking. Zmuda, Kuklis, and Kline (2004), in *Transforming Schools: Creating a Culture of Continuous Improvement*, describe that as

- The school as a system of interlocking and interacting elements
- The beliefs and behavioral norms that define a culture and their role in promoting or blocking change
- The need for collegiality (p. 31)

How those items interlace in your particular setting will be for you and your staff to determine. Each school culture is different, and there is no one recipe for success. However, the leader can provide the focus, the opportunity, and the discussions that lead to student achievement.

A Possible System of Accountability

I have a way to hold schools—all schools—accountable without holding them hostage. Right now, we pay schools based on the number of students. We pay them no matter what a student has learned or what mastery level a student has achieved.

What if schools were paid when students achieved a year's worth of growth in reading, math, and science, instead of being paid on seat time? Right now, our schools are more concerned with social promotion than achievement. If we did not receive state aid until students learned, and the students could not move forward until that happened, we would truly hold schools accountable. And here is the best part: If students cannot read, for example, they would not be passed on until they could. We would have ungraded classrooms so that students would be taught at their instructional level. We would have teachers who are trained to teach certain skills, teaching them to students at that learning level, regardless of age. The emphasis would be on learning, not age. It's almost like the old-fashioned country schools, using nongraded classrooms, peer tutors, and students learning at their instructional level.

Some students might graduate by the time they were age 16, maybe even 13, and others would stay until they were age 21.

It would not matter because students would learn, and schools would be held accountable.

To make this system work, we would have to give up the paradigm of graded schools, going to the next grade based on chronological age instead of mastery of content, and funding based on numbers of students enrolled on a certain date.

What Does an Administrator Need to Do?

1. Be familiar with the laws of the NCLB and state mandates. There are Web sites galore to assist. One federal Web site, www .ed.gov, stays current with the federal laws. Your own state has a Web site that will have information regarding your own state standards, testing schedules, and reporting requirements.

2. Acquire some tools for managing data. If you did not have any formal training in undergraduate or graduate school, pick up some books on looking at, interpreting, and using data. There are many resources. *Using Data to Improve Schools: What's Working* (American Association of School Administrators, 2004), for example, is a short, very helpful book. Another author whom I find to be particularly helpful is Victoria L. Bernhardt, PhD, who wrote *Data Analysis for Continuous School Improvement* (2004). There are many, many more.

3. Use data and discussions around data as jumping-off points to becoming a professional learning community. Richard DuFour, former principal and superintendent of Stevenson High School in Illinois, has published a book (DuFour & Eaker, 1998) about professional learning communities. He writes for the National Staff Development Council (NSDC) and speaks throughout the country on the topic.

True professional learning communities have a professional topic to discuss and learn. Data, analyzing student progress, learning different instructional strategies to meet individual learning needs, and other such topics are topics for grade-level teams, departments, schools, and districts as they establish a community that is reflective and active in their desire to improve.

4. Understand the role of professional development. Some teachers may be fearful of using data that are specific to their students because they do not want to be compared with others. They are so fearful of being perceived as a failure. However, if the discussions are

led in a nonthreatening manner, they create a learning community where teachers and students alike are winners.

When looking at student performance, particularly if there is a data drill-down tool that can actually track performance by teacher, some people will be afraid that they are not doing enough. But what we know as educators is that not all children are the same, not all classes are the same, and not all grade cohorts are the same. This year's fifth graders are different from next year's, and a teacher's individual class is different from the class down the hall.

It is important to create a nonthreatening, nonjudgmental atmosphere where teachers can learn from one another. It may be necessary to provide some targeted training in areas where people need it. No one person can know everything. That is why we have professional development. So, as conversations progress, one of the questions can always be, "What do we need to know for this to happen? What professional development do we need?" And then make that happen.

5. Keep accountability in perspective. Public schools are to provide a free, public, comprehensive education. Do not become so immersed in data and test scores that you forget the big picture and the moral obligation connected with the purpose of a free public comprehensive education.

Those who have traveled outside of the United States to less developed parts of the world are constantly reminded that one of the reasons this country is great is because of its gem of a free, public, comprehensive education. The American Association of School Administrators (2004) reminds us that "there may be another mission that is completely overlooked in the consideration of universal high achievement—developing citizens to maintain the democracy—that is critical to equal opportunity and thus universal high achievement."

Students need music and reading. They need physical education and math. They need to learn about the role of a citizen in maintaining democracy for the benefit of all. It is important to keep perspective.

What we are learning as a nation is that most parents, when given an option to leave their neighborhood schools, do not do so. Public opinion, as shown in Phi Delta Kappa polls that are conducted every year, is that schools do a good job, even if people believe that other schools in the nation do not. Make certain that parents are informed about what is happening in each building. What gains are your students making? Where do you need more work? What does the state report card mean? How can they help? Work with the district communications person, if you have one, to have public discussions and communications.

6. Be an ethical and moral leader. We have to make certain that our students are learning. We have to follow the letter of the law. However, if we believe something is wrong, we can work to correct it. If you have an issue with the accountability system, be vocal to your union, state department, and federal legislators. Write letters. Make telephone calls.

Also, keep in mind that our mission is to provide a free, public, comprehensive education for all students. It is our job to be moral, ethical leaders. Be reflective with staff and have a discussion about what that means. Michael Hartoonian, professor at the University of Minnesota, Minneapolis, gave a keynote speech to social studies teachers in 2003. He told the story of ships on the high seas in the days of wind-powered vessels. As ships met, they asked each other three questions: Who is your captain? What is your cargo? Where are you going?

As an ethical leader, ask yourself and your staff the following: Who is your captain? What is your cargo? Where are you going?

SUMMARY

No one objects to being held accountable. However, all entities should be held accountable equally—private, public, charter, and home schools.

Use measures that look at growth, not comparing this year's fourth grade to next year's fourth grade, which is statistically irrelevant.

Establish a professional learning community in the truest sense of the words, where teachers and students alike are learning and growing.

Box 11.1 Journal

1. How am I moving my staff forward to build a learning community for adults and students alike?

2. Other ideas from the chapter. . . .

C H A P T E R   T W E L V E

Becoming a Self-Assured Administrator

W ho said being an administrator would be fun? I did. It is a career that offers the opportunity to affect the future of our students and our country. Educators, whether teachers or administrators, are in a profession that has a high degree of moral purpose. As Fullan (1993) stated, "Managing moral purpose and change agentry is at the heart of productive educational change" (p. 8). Goodlad, as quoted in Fullan (1993, p. 9), describes four "moral imperatives" that are part of that moral purpose, because schools and the people who lead them are

- "The only institution in our nation specifically charged with enculturating the young into a political democracy"
- "The only institution in our society specifically charged with providing to the young a disciplined encounter with all the subject matters of the human conversation"
- Willing to go beyond the *mechanics* of teaching to build effective teacher-student connections
- Engaging teachers purposefully in the renewal process

The profession is paradoxical because of the following:

- Although tasks are completed daily, the work is never *done.*
- As society changes, we must change with it but keep the importance of the past.
- We must be super-communicators, and the more one communicates with e-mail, voice mail, and faxes, the more that is expected.
- An administrator is supposed to be self-aware so it is easier to deal with personalities of students, staff, and parents. Yet, an administrator cannot be too involved or it is seen as a frailty.
- Administrators are supposed to be instructional leaders, but daily management needs leave them little time for this.
- Administrators have to be aware of and enforce a "bottom line" in finance, personnel issues, discipline, and building management but must use *process* to facilitate change.

Being an administrator is exhausting, yet exhilarating, and challenging, yet rewarding. But it is a job that makes a difference. It matters. It counts, which is exactly why being a school administrator *is* fun.

References

American Association of School Administrators. (2004). *Using data to improve schools: What's working.* Arlington, VA: Author. Accessed from www.aasa.org/about/SUPE_brief.htm

Bernhardt, V. L. (2004). *Data analysis for continuous school improvement.* Larchmont, NY: Eye on Education.

Bolman, L. G., & Deal, T. E. (1991). *Reframing organizations: Artistry, choice, and leadership.* San Francisco: Jossey-Bass.

Boyum, R. (n.d.). *Characteristics of healthy relationships in healthy organizations.* Retrieved September 25, 2004, from www.uwec.edu/counsel/pubs/healthyorg.html

Bozarth-Campbell, A. (1982). *Life is goodbye, life is hello.* Minneapolis, MN: Compcare.

Bracey, G. W. (2003). *What you need to know about the war against America's public schools.* Needham Heights, MA: Allyn & Bacon.

Brighouse, T., & Woods, D. (1999). *How to improve your school.* London: Routledge & Falmer.

Collins, J. (2001). *Good to great.* New York: HarperCollins.

Cousins, N. (1979). *Anatomy of an illness.* New York: Bantam.

Cuban, L. (2001). *How can I fix it? Finding solutions and managing dilemmas.* New York: Teachers College Press.

Cuban, L., & Tyack, D. (1995). *Tinkering toward Utopia.* Cambridge, MA: Harvard University Press.

DuFour, R., & Eaker, R. (1998). *Professional learning communities at work: Best practices for enhancing student achievement.* Bloomington, IN: National Education Service.

Fielder, D. (2003). *Achievement now: How to assure no child is left behind.* Larchmont, NY: Eye on Education.

Fisher, R., Ury, W., & Patton, B. (1991). *Getting to yes: Negotiating agreement without giving in.* New York: Penguin.

French, J. R. P., & Raven, B. (1959). *Bases of social power: Studies in social power.* Ann Arbor: University of Michigan Press.

Fullan, M. (1993). *Change forces: Probing the depths of educational reform.* London: Falmer.

Fullan, M. (2001). *The new meaning of educational change.* New York: Teachers College Press.

Garmston, R. J., & Wellman, B. M. (1999). *The adaptive school: A sourcebook for developing collaborative groups.* Norwood, MA: Christopher-Gordon.

Hall, G. E., & Hord, S. M. (2001). *Implementing change: Patterns, principles, and potholes.* Needham Heights, MA: Allyn & Bacon.

Hanh, T. N. (1998). *The heart of the Buddha's teaching.* New York: Broadway.

Hartoonian, M. (September, 2002). The Moral Responsibility of Public Education. Presentation at Wayzata High School.

James, J. (1996). *Thinking in the future tense.* New York: Touchstone.

Kubler-Ross, E. (1969). *On death and dying.* New York: Touchstone.

LaRoche, L. (1998). *Relax, you may only have a few minutes left.* New York: Villard.

Levinson, D. J. (1978). *The seasons of a man's life.* New York: Ballantine.

Lieb, S. (n.d.). *Principles of adult learning.* Retrieved September 25, 2004, from http://honolulu.hawaii.edu/intranet/committees/FacDevCom/guidebk/teachtip/adults-2.htm

Palmer, P. J. (1998). *The courage to teach: Exploring the inner landscape of a teacher's life.* San Francisco: Jossey-Bass.

Pipher, M. (2002). *The middle of everywhere: Helping refugees enter the American community.* Orlando, FL: Harcourt.

Rogers, J. (2001). *Innovation adoption in Value-Based Management.net.* Retrieved September 25, 2004, from www.valuebasedmanagement.net/methods_rogers_innovation_adoption_curve.html

Second law of thermodynamics. (n.d.). Retrieved September 25, 2004, from ww.emc.maricopa.edu/faculty/farabee/BIOBK/BioBookEner1.html

Sheehy, G. (1997). *Passages: Predictable crises of adult life.* New York: Dutton. (Original work published 1974)

Siegel, B. (1998). *Love, medicine, and miracles.* New York: Quill.

Sigford, J. L. (1995). *Self-determinants of success by the women who are head principals of high schools in Minnesota.* Unpublished doctoral dissertation, University of Minnesota, Minneapolis.

Strauss, W., & Howe, N. (1991). *Generations: The history of America's future, 1584 to 2069.* New York: Quill, Morrow.

Strauss, W., & Howe, N. (1997). *The fourth turning: What the cycles of history tell us about America's next rendezvous with destiny.* New York: Broadway.

Tyack, D. B., & Strober, M. H. (1981). *Women and men in the schools: A history of the sexual structuring of educational employment.* Paper prepared for the National Institute of Education, Washington, D.C.

Ury, W. (1991). *Getting past no: Negotiating with difficult people.* New York: Bantam.

Wheatley, M. J. (1994). *Leadership and the new science: Learning about organization from an orderly universe.* San Francisco: Berrett-Koehler.

Whitaker, T. (1999). *Dealing with difficult teachers.* New York: Eye on Education.

Whitaker, T., & Fiore, D. J. (2001). *Dealing with difficult parents (and with parents in a difficult situation).* New York: Eye on Education.

Young, P. G. (2004). *You have to go to school—you're the principal.* Thousand Oaks, CA: Corwin.

Zemke, R, Raines, C., & Filipczak, B. (2000). *Generations at work: Managing the clash of veterans, boomers, Xers, and Nexters in your workplace.* New York: AMACOM.

Zmuda, A., Kuklis, R., & Kline, E. (2004). *Transforming schools: Creating a culture of continuous improvement.* Alexandria, VA: ASCD.

Index